STRAIGHT UP

OR ON THE ROCKS

STRAIGHT UP

OR ON THE ROCKS

THE STORY OF THE AMERICAN COCKTAIL

WILLIAM GRIMES

NORTH POINT PRESS

A DIVISION OF FARRAR, STRAUS AND GIROUX

NEW YORK

North Point Press
A division of Farrar, Straus and Giroux
19 Union Square West, New York 10003

Distributed in Canada by Douglas & McIntyre Ltd.
Printed in the United States of America
Original edition published in 1993 by Simon & Schuster
First revised edition, North Point Press, 2001

Library of Congress Cataloging-in-Publication Data
Grimes, William.
    Straight up or on the rocks : the story of the American cocktail /
William Grimes.
        p.   cm.
    Includes bibliographical references and index.
    ISBN 0-86547-601-2 (hc. : alk. paper)
    1. Cocktails.   2. Alcoholic beverages—United States—History.
I. Title.
TX951.G7867 2001
641.8'74—dc21

                                                            2001032987

Designed by Jonathan D. Lippincott

TO NANCY

Perhaps it's made of whiskey and perhaps it's made of gin,
Perhaps there's orange bitters and a lemon peel within,
Perhaps it's called Martini and perhaps it's called, again,
The name that spread Manhattan's fame among the sons of men;
Perhaps you like it garnished with what thinking men avoid,
The little blushing cherry that is made of celluloid,
But be these matters as they may, a *cher confrère* you are
If you admire the cocktail they pass along the bar.

—Wallace Irwin, "The Great American Cocktail,"
San Francisco News Letter, March 8, 1902

CONTENTS

PREFACE

National genius is almost by definition indefinable. It's as likely to reside in a colorful turn of phrase, a facial expression, or a culinary quirk as it is in the grand events we normally think of as history. No one would argue that the French Revolution was less than epoch-making, but France expresses its Frenchness more immediately, and just as persuasively, in a glass of burgundy or an enthusiasm for obscure Hollywood directors. These are the parts that add up to a much greater whole, the small but colorful fish that slip through the historian's net.

The United States, too, expresses its character in a thousand seemingly trivial but potent messages, unremarked upon by the natives themselves but instantly perceived by outsiders. One of them is the cocktail.

America could be described as the country where people mix their drinks in strange, tantalizing combinations and then consume them ice-cold. It is the land of the brave and the home of the martini.

This sounds flip (the name of a colonial drink, by the way).

We would like the world to admire us for the Bill of Rights or the Marshall Plan. But cultural influence doesn't work that way. No one admires an abstraction. Or more precisely, the admiration one feels for an abstraction tends to be abstract; genuine emotion feeds on particulars.

For most of the world, America is the great entertainment factory. The New Jerusalem envisioned by the Puritans has turned out to be the world's leading manufacturer of idle amusement and cheap thrills. The colonists and their descendants did indeed build them a shining city on a hill—but they called it Disneyland. In the Declaration of Independence they enshrined, along with life and liberty, the inalienable right to pursue happiness. But happiness is hard. Happiness takes work. Even worse, happiness is a long shot. So America settled for fun, perfected it, and sold it to an eager world. Pop music, Hollywood movies, the seductive sound of ice chattering in a silver cocktail shaker—these are the tangible, consumable expressions of the lofty principles in the Declaration of Independence, the free culture of a free people.

This is a roundabout way of saying that the cocktail is more than a drink. It may not be, as H. L. Mencken called it, "the greatest of all the contributions of the American way of life to the salvation of mankind," but it remains a durable, deeply appealing component of Americanness, born of experiment and ingenuity, and, like all authentic art forms, inexhaustible and infinitely adaptable. Mencken once claimed that he and a friend hired a mathematician to compute how many cocktails could be made from the ingredients available at a respectable bar. The total was 17,864,392,788. "We tried 273 at random," he reported, "and found them all good."

Thousands of new cocktails have appeared since Mencken commissioned his study. The Sage of Baltimore did not live to see the Fuzzy Navel, the Screaming Orgasm, or the Teeny Weeny Woo Woo, and perhaps it's just as well. But he would have understood the manic inventiveness behind the Slippery Nipple and similar drinks. As a locus for pure invention and a symbol of modernity, the cocktail glass cannot be equaled. It is a glass-enclosed void in which anything can happen, a restless, anxiety-tinged emptiness, a never-ending text forever spinning off new readings, a vacuum that absorbs the humming, buzzing signals of the world's most restless culture. It's no accident that the neon martini glass, effulgent symbol of the American bar, is always empty.

This profound instability and waywardness lie at the cocktail's very heart. It is radical by birth. Although historians often point out that the colonial tavern was a cradle of the Revolution, they neglect to mention that it was in the tavern that Americans first began disturbing the established hierarchies of wine and spirits, mixing and fixing with whatever alcoholic and flavoring materials lay ready to hand. From these seemingly random efforts developed a purely American notion of the drink as a continually evolving work in progress.

The drinks of the Old World, seemingly as ancient as root and soil, reflected a fixed social order and the attendant values of homogeneity, cohesion, and tradition. They still do. European efforts to break loose and embrace the cocktail have always been self-consciously American—a French bar specializing in cocktails is called a *bar américain*—and less than convincing. The spirit may be willing, but in fundamental matters like drink, national currents run strong and deep. The French poet Paul Claudel once remarked, "A cocktail is to a glass of wine as rape is to love." It's hard to break the hold of a sentiment like that.

Small wonder that Europe has taken an academic approach

to the cocktail, regarding it as a compelling but inscrutable ar-
tifact, like an African mask. In 1973, a bartender at the Savoy
Hotel in London decided to celebrate Britain's entry into the
European Economic Community by creating a new cocktail,
the Common Market. It was equal parts Elixir d'Anu (Bel-
gium), Cherry Heering (Denmark), dry vermouth (France),
Schlichte (West Germany), sloe gin (Britain), curaçao (the
Netherlands), dry white wine (Luxembourg), coffee liqueur
(Ireland), and Punt è Mes (Italy). This nightmare of pedantry
was served at the hotel's American bar, and it's a safe bet that
no one ever ordered one except on a dare. The Common Market is not a drink, it's a bureaucratic document.

You can't blame Europe for trying. Wherever the cocktail
has appeared, it has had a beneficial, loosening effect on social
customs. Alec Waugh, brother of Evelyn, described the cocktail's ascendancy in England in the 1920s, a time when the
awkward period of pre-dinner socializing was known as *le
mauvais quart d'heure*. The mixed drink came as a godsend,
and England's flaming youth grabbed for it with both hands,
especially the champagne cocktail. (For the results, consult the
novels of Evelyn Waugh, passim.) But as with jazz, appreciation never sparked invention. Professional bartenders' organi-
zations were formed, combining the attributes of a medieval
craft guild and the Académie Française. They organized tour-
naments of skill, resulting in champion cocktails every bit as
good as the Common Market.

Americans approached the cocktail in the same spirit as
they did popular art forms like the newspaper cartoon strip or
the Tin Pan Alley song, driven by imagination, exuberance,
and the profit motive. From the beginning, there has been a
tendency to err on the side of excess. The flashy, vulgar drink
has always been with us. True to the Hollywood ratio, there are

a hundred execrable cocktails for every classic, but without the awful drinks, the classics would not exist. And the classics could not have been invented anywhere but in the United States.

This has something to do with a peculiarity of American society that foreigners often sense but cannot fully understand. The free and easy, gregarious American social style disguises a profound detachment and sense of solitude. The surface warmth that outsiders immediately notice belies a coolness within. This is part of the Faustian bargain that America has made to gain freedom and riches. We breathe a freer but harsher air. Along with the constraints that made the towns of the Old World suffocating and restrictive, our forebears threw off the warm blanket of custom, mutual obligation, and rootedness.

Competitive and mobile, Americans have had to develop social forms that promote quick, effortless acquaintance rather than lasting bonds. In no other society are strangers who have grown up thousands of miles apart more likely to be thrown together and expected not only to get along and do business, but to regard one another as friends. Hence the cocktail party, more often than not a gathering of near-strangers brought together in a setting of false intimacy.

The cocktail stands for sociability with no strings attached. It is shallow; but it is also profound. A glass in hand, ice cubes tinkling, can suggest hilarity, a crowded room, and social adventure. Or it can evoke the solitary man at the end of the bar, lost in thought, staring into the plumbless depths of a four-ounce glass.

Cold, clean, slightly astringent, the cocktail represents a decisive break with the preindustrial past, when liquors were seen as a kind of food, warm and nourishing. Falstaff's red nose

and enormous belly testified to the combustive, nutritive pow-
ers of ale and sack. Smollett's roisterers rallied round the silver
bowl brimming with fumacious, scalding punch. Boswell and
Johnson found inspiration in their nightly ration of two bottles
of port. Heat, fat, solidity, weight—these are the key Old
World attributes assigned to drink.

Consider one of the great cocktail drinkers of the modern
age, James Bond. Although patriotic, Bond is in fundamental
respects very un-English. The first Transatlantic Man, he is
perfectly at home with advanced technology, flashy gadgets,
and foreign languages. Significantly, he asserts his identity
through highly chilled, distinctive cocktails; he even invents
his own. M., his boss, sticks to whiskey at his club, Blades.
Bond's peculiar drinking habits are as alien to M. as his fast
cars, faster women, and razor-sharp suits. With his vodka martinis, Bond announces, in effect, *I am modern, therefore American.*

The triumph of the cocktail did not come overnight. Like the
United States itself, the drink began as an Anglo-American hy-
brid, struggled to find a native form, achieved full maturity in
the late nineteenth century, and today flourishes thanks to
myriad international influences, most of them from the third
world. As the cocktail goes, so goes the nation.

And vice versa. The cocktail has now entered a more
thoughtful, reflective, even self-conscious phase, the result of
moderated drinking habits. To the despair of the spirits industry, Americans, by international standards always a rather ab-
stemious people, are drinking still less these days. The
downward trend began about fifteen years ago and shows no
signs of slowing. Despite cheering news about the beneficial

effects of red wine on the heart, Americans now tend to see drinking as a health hazard. Law and public opinion take a harsh view of drunken driving, and rightly so. Public intoxication does not seem quite as amusing as it did a few decades back, when the three-martini lunch was standard. *Three martinis?* What race of giants roamed the earth in those far-off days? Easier to picture Paul Bunyan felling an ox with one fist. Today's business lunch is lubricated with sparkling mineral water enlivened with a slice of lime. In a wild mood, the modern executive might order a glass of chilled chardonnay.

Somewhat paradoxically, moderation seems to have inspired a kind of connoisseurship. Even as consumption declines, interest in the fine points of wine and spirits has picked up, if only for practical reasons. If you're going to drink less, why not drink better? And if you're going to drink better—to move up from *cru bourgeois* to second growth, from blended Scotch to a recherché single malt—doesn't it pay to know more about what you're pouring into the glass? Knowledge has a way of feeding on its own appetite, and soon natural curiosity takes over. Where did the Bronx and the Sidecar come from? What on earth was the Zaza cocktail? Was the martini always dry, and how did it get its name in the first place? This book grew out of questions like these, and the belief that even if firm answers would be hard to come by, the search would make for creative browsing along the way.

"Cocktail" sounds like a wily game bird. It acts like one too. It can be glimpsed only fleetingly, at the margins of history, turning up in the short descriptive passage of a traveler, the offhand remark of a fictional character, the unembellished report of a journalist. As the temperance movement gained strength in the United States, references to drink, other than as a problem, virtually disappeared from the printed record. With few exceptions, America's notoriously hard-drinking novelists ignored the glass in their hand, failing to recognize it as a piece of social information as revealing as clothing style, accent, or occupation. The cocktail has been, so to speak, everywhere and nowhere. Back in the 1930s, G. Selmer Fougner used to issue calls for cocktail recipes in his column in the *New York Sun*, "Along the Wine Trail." On one occasion, four hundred readers responded to his request for the correct ingredients in a Ward 8. Today, perhaps half that number even know that the Ward 8 is a drink.

A sense of history also pervades this book's recipes, which were subjected to ruthless winnowing. Most cocktails, like most plays or paintings, are bad. The standard cocktail book, ignoring this sad fact, offers hundreds of recipes regardless of merit. The encyclopedic approach makes sense in a book intended for bartenders, but for the rest of us, profusion equals confusion. This book includes more than one hundred recipes, selected according to the principle of benevolent elitism. It presents the classics and worthy variations thereof, as well as deserving drinks that have somehow fallen out of favor over the decades. In other words, breeding counts. But talent does too. The American cocktail is nothing if not forward-looking and optimistic. Accordingly, my list includes a goodly number of new and innovative cocktails, served at America's best bars, restaurants, and hotels. The door slams shut, however, on the flashy newcomer—the fellow with the loud suit and the back-slapping manner. He has been directed to that singles bar down the road, where the drinks come in fun colors and go out of fashion in a week.

What makes a great cocktail? For that matter, what is a cocktail? The word first appeared in 1806, conveniently enough in the form of a definition. The editor of the Hudson,

New York, *Balance and Columbian Repository*, responding to a perplexed reader's query, wrote: "Cocktail is a stimulating liquor, composed of spirits of any kind, sugar, water, and bitters." Substitute ice for water, and the definition holds up pretty well. But even the slimmest cocktail book will contain exceptions. It's consistent with the negative logic of the cocktail that if a drink cannot be proven *not* to be a cocktail, it is one. Quibblers can parse the differences between a cocktail and an aperitif, but that way madness lies. Strictly speaking, a Manhattan is a cocktail, not a before-dinner appetite enhancer, but in practice Americans drink all sorts of things before, during, and after a meal and would probably call every one of them a cocktail if it was cold and had some spirit as a base. "Cocktail" and "mixed drink" have often been synonymous, yet cocktails have on occasion been pared down to a single ingredient. So: Scotch with ice cubes—yes. White wine with ice cubes—no. The Jell-O Shot, a vodka-laced cube of flavored gelatin served in a little paper cup—no, no, no.

Abominations like the Jell-O Shot remind us that standards do matter. Common sense and custom suggest that a cocktail should be cold and snappy. It should be invigorating to the palate and pleasing to the eye. That covers most of the territory. A rare few, like the daiquiri and the martini, combine their minimal ingredients to achieve, in a magical synthesis, an entirely new flavor. Others are content to play beguiling variations on a theme. Still others, like the highball, don't do much of anything at all except refresh. But these too have their place in the grand scheme.

Whatever a cocktail's ingredients, the whole should add up to more than the sum of the parts. And the parts should coexist in a state of balance—what the old Charles Atlas ads called "Dynamic Tension." No single ingredient should overpower the others. The bartender who pours with a heavy hand does the customer no favor if he throws the entire cocktail out of joint.

A good cocktail, properly mixed, should lift the spirits, refresh the mind, and put into healthy perspective the countless worries and grievances of modern life. The fretful neurotic who shakes up an after-work martini should emerge from the experience a changed human being: more generous and sociable, inclined toward deeper thought and the pleasures of the imagination. In that mood, Martini Man might spare a thought for the anonymous tavern keepers and bartenders of the past 350 years, the humble inventors who brought to perfection this unheralded branch of the culinary arts. America has given the world much. It should take pride in the cocktail too.

—

STRAIGHT UP

OR ON THE ROCKS

ONE

THE MARTINI

There is a point at which the marriage of gin and vermouth is consummated. It varies a little with the con-
stituents, but for a gin of 94.4 proof and a harmonious
vermouth it may be generalized at about 3.7 to one.
—Bernard DeVoto, *The Hour* (1946)

Human invention has launched untold thousands of cocktails,
but only one has developed a genuine mystique: the martini. It
is the quintessential cocktail, the standard by which all others
are judged. Immune to shifting taste and fashion, the martini
has not only endured, it has prospered. The Jack Rose, the
Sidecar, the Bronx, where are they now? Those tasty mainstays
of the 1930s and 1940s survive only as period pieces. Yet the
martini maintains its steady course, a blue-chip investment
paying out the same handsome dividend year after year.

Let the martini serve as a touchstone for this book, a North
Star by which to navigate the bewildering world of mixed
drinks. And just as surveys of Western art begin with an inspi-
rational discourse on the Acropolis or *Winged Victory*, let this

rambling tour of American drink begin with the epitome of cocktail perfection.

For the true martini believer, the combination of gin, vermouth, and olive is the Holy Trinity. And like any theological principle, it has given rise to doctrinal dispute. Put two worshipers together in the same room, and the arguments begin. Points of contention include, but are not limited to, the proper ingredients and their ideal proportions, the fastest way to achieve maximum coldness, and the merits of shaking versus stirring. Should a glass pitcher or a metal shaker be used? Should the olive have a pimento or not? These are matters of faith, not reason, for the martini is a cult, perhaps a religion. It even has its martyr, Sherwood Anderson, who succumbed to peritonitis after swallowing the toothpick from a martini olive. Consider him a sacrifice to the Egyptian god of thirst, Dri Mart Ini, whose cult was described by "Percival Slathers" in the *New York Sun* seventy-five years ago. The god, he wrote, was depicted by ancient artists as a priest of Isis, "shaking a drink in a covered urn of glass while the 15th pharaoh of the dynasty of Lush is shown with protruding cottony tongue quivering with pleasurable expectation."

Just how the martini got its name remains a mystery. Trying to solve it leads the hapless etymologist down one of the most meandering paths in the English language. The British long assumed that the drink originated with the Martini & Henry rifle, used throughout the Empire and known for its strong kick. Italians have argued, plausibly enough, that the name comes from Martini & Rossi vermouth. Both are wrong. The drink predates the rifle. And it was popular long before Martini & Rossi vermouth showed up on these shores. If the drink were named after a vermouth, Noilly Prat would be the one. Lowell Edmunds, in *Martini, Straight Up*, found that it was being exported to the United States as early as the 1850s.

Most Americans are wrong about the birth of the martini too; but somewhat more interestingly, they are wrong in two different ways. Over the years, two schools of thought on the time and place of the martini's origin have evolved, which, for convenience, we can label the West Coast and the East Coast hypotheses. Let us consider each in turn.

The West Coast hypothesis, to make matters more complicated, divides into two minor hypotheses, the San Francisco and the Martinez. The former holds that the renowned bartender Jerry Thomas, author of the first known cocktail book, mixed gin and vermouth for the first time at San Francisco's Occidental Hotel in the 1860s. His lucky customer, legend has it, was a traveler bound for nearby Martinez. With time, the Martinez cocktail became the martini. (The first recipe under the word "martini" appears in an 1888 bar guide by Harry Johnson.) The citizens of Martinez maintain that the first martini drinker was a gold miner who, in the 1870s, dropped by the bar of Julio Richelieu, a French immigrant whose improbable first name has never been explained. The traveler bought a bottle of whiskey for the road, paid with a gold nugget, and instead of change asked for a brand-new cocktail on the spot. He got it, and Richelieu called it the Martinez.

Both hypotheses rest on sand. For one thing, the Martinez makes its first appearance not in Jerry Thomas's book, published in 1862, but in an 1884 bar guide by O. H. Byron, who described the drink as a Manhattan in which gin is substituted for whiskey. If Thomas invented the drink, he mysteriously omitted it from the first edition of his *How to Mix Drinks*, subtitled *The Bon-Vivant's Companion*. It does not show up until the much-expanded 1887 edition of the book, and it's clear that no one arguing the San Francisco hypothesis has ever looked at the recipe. Thomas's Martinez cocktail called for one ounce of Old Tom gin, one wineglass (!) of vermouth, two dashes of maraschino, one dash of bitters, and two small lumps of ice, with sugar syrup added to taste.

Is this really a martini? True, there's vermouth, but Thomas had in mind the sweet red Italian variety. There's gin, but again, it's the wrong kind. Old Tom gin, a rarity nowadays, has sugar added during distillation. Thomas's martini is a molten gumdrop, although it must be remembered that many nineteenth-century cocktails reflect a national sweet tooth. Much closer to the mark is Thomas's 1862 recipe for a gin cocktail, which calls for gin, curaçao, bitters, and sugar syrup, garnished with a twist of lemon. Take away the syrup, add sweet vermouth, and you get the martini recipe that held sway into the early twentieth century. It is, in fact, the Martinez recipe we find in Byron's *Modern Bartender's Guide* (1884). To complicate the picture, two cocktails that seem to be close cousins of the dry martini show up in bar guides around the turn of the century, the Marguerite (Plymouth gin and French vermouth with a dash of orange bitters) and the Puritan (Plymouth gin, French vermouth, and orange bitters with a splash of yellow Chartreuse).

The East Coast hypothesis holds that Martini di Arma di Taggia, a bartender at the Knickerbocker Hotel in New York, created a drink using equal parts gin and dry vermouth some-time after arriving in America in 1912. That date would make di Taggia a straggler in the race, since several bar books and contemporary accounts show that the martini was already well established by the 1880s. But wait. Those early martinis, like Thomas's Martinez, used Italian vermouth. So di Taggia could be the man. On the other hand, William F. Mulhall, a veteran bartender, wrote of serving martinis at New York's swanky Hoffman House in the 1880s, and although he did not specify ingredients or proportions, he did refer to both sweet and dry martinis as among the most popular cocktails of the day.

By today's standards, which call for one part vermouth to anywhere between five and fifteen parts gin, the Knickerbocker martini was sickly sweet, but it definitely bears the distinctive markings of the breed. After all, a ratio of three parts vermouth to one part gin was typical as recently as the 1930s, when *Esquire* was recommending Italian vermouth for a medium martini and equal parts French and Italian vermouth for a semidry martini. One of the great cultural shocks still available in this age of jet travel and instant communication is the experience of ordering a martini in an English pub. The wretch who makes this mistake will receive a small glass of sweet vermouth. A request for a dry martini will elicit a small glass of French vermouth. The only fail-safe method is to ask for a "gin and French" with ice.

Gradually the martini became drier. Somewhere along the way it achieved greatness. As *New Yorker* readers cannot help but know, the drink (like the magazine) has for generations been a kind of tribal totem for the East Coast business establishment. Its power as a symbol lives on, well past the era of its actual dominance. One characteristic cartoon in the magazine showed two cavemen, returning from the hunt, carrying three giant olives impaled on a pole, their destination a giant martini glass. (On Madison Avenue, the martini was referred to, depending on the garnish, as a deep-dish olive, lemon, or onion pie.) But the martini's fame extends far beyond traditional WASP watering holes. The triangular glass with an olive in it has been adopted as the international symbol for "bar." It is the only cocktail to have made the leap from drink to symbol.

It is also the only cocktail to have inspired books. Lowell Edmunds, a classics professor at Rutgers University, produced a treatise devoted entirely to the martini. Originally titled *The Silver Bullet*, after one of the martini's nicknames, it was recently revised and retitled *Martini, Straight Up*. The book, a blend of careful scholarship, ingenuity, and enthusiasm, explores what Edmunds calls the "ambiguities" of the martini. The drink, he argues, is at once civilized and uncivilized, connoting sophistication but also excess. It is sensitive yet tough. It can be bruised, yet its potency is legendary.

Perhaps most beguiling, the martini is both classic and individual, public and private. As a two-ingredient drink, it should logically have a set form pleasing to all martini drinkers, yet it seems to demand endless tinkering. It is the cock-

---

To provoke, or sustain, a reverie in a bar, you have to drink English gin, especially in the form of the dry martini. To be frank, given the primordial role played in my life by the dry martini, I think I really ought to give it at least a page. Like all cocktails, the martini, composed essentially of gin and a few drops of Noilly Prat, seems to have been an American invention. Connoisseurs who like their martinis very dry suggest simply allowing a ray of sunlight to shine through a bottle of Noilly Prat before it hits the bottle of gin. At a certain period in America it was said that the making of a dry martini should resemble the Immaculate Conception, for, as Saint Thomas Aquinas once noted, the generative power of the Holy Ghost pierced the Virgin's hymen "like a ray of sunlight through a window—leaving it unbroken."

Another crucial recommendation is that the ice be so cold and hard that it won't melt, since nothing's worse than a watery martini. For those who are still with me, let me give you my personal recipe, the fruit of long experimentation and guaranteed to produce perfect results. The day before your guests arrive, put all the ingredients—glasses, gin, and shaker—in the refrigerator. Use a thermometer to make sure the ice is

tail of a thousand idiosyncrasies. Every martini devotee believes that he has a particular variant or technical refinement that makes the drink his own, yet it always remains a martini. The reason for this is not hard to find. The martini induces a meditative state, and meditation promotes a deep personal bond between the drinker and the drink.

Some of the variants are perverse. Stalin downed one of FDR's martinis at the Teheran Conference in 1943, pronouncing it very good, but "cold on the stomach." He was being polite. Roosevelt's recipe, provided to a persistent radio reporter named Jack Reed, called for two parts gin to one part vermouth, with a teaspoon of olive brine. It was served with an olive and, "for extra smoothness," the rim of the glass was rubbed with lemon peel. The result was noisome but perhaps

---

about twenty degrees below zero (centigrade). Don't take anything out until your friends arrive; then pour a few drops of Noilly Prat and half a demitasse spoon of Angostura bitters over the ice. Shake it, then pour it out, keeping only the ice, which retains a faint taste of both. Then pour straight gin over the ice, shake it again, and serve.

(During the 1940s, the director of the Museum of Modern Art in New York taught me a curious variation. Instead of Angostura, he used a dash of Pernod. Frankly, it seemed heretical to me, but apparently it was only a fad.)

After the dry martini comes one of my own modest inventions, the Buñueloni, best drunk before dinner. It's really a takeoff on the famous Negroni, but instead of mixing Campari, gin, and sweet Cinzano, I substitute Carpano for the Campari. Here again, the gin—in sufficient quantity to ensure its dominance over the other two ingredients—has excellent effects on the imagination. I've no idea how or why; I only know that it works.

—Luis Buñuel, *My Last Sigh* (1982)

diplomatically effective, since one administration official char-
acterized U.S.-Soviet relations under Roosevelt as the "four
martinis and let's have an agreement" era. So now we know
where to put the blame for Yalta.

The personal approach in martini mixing always provokes
an equal and opposite countertheory. Always, an expert is on
hand. Paul Farley, in John O'Hara's *Butterfield 8*, explains that
he used to worry about bruising the gin if he shook his martinis, until he was converted by a contemptuous English bartender: "He told me a Martini ought to be shaken very hard,
briskly, a few vigorous shakes up and down, so that the gin and
vermouth would be cracked into a proper *foamy* mixture." The
alleged advantage here is that the drink becomes aerated and
therefore less potent, making it possible to polish off several.

This is pure nonsense. Try shaking a martini. Shake it for
an hour, or several days, if you like, and see if anything like
foam appears. It doesn't. O'Hara's martini is a literary artifact,
the direct descendant of the martini with "the smooth infini-
tesimal foam" that makes a cameo appearance in Dos Passos's
Manhattan Transfer.

Edmunds also found in the martini a number of unam-
biguous messages. It is American. It is urban, upper-class, and
male. It is nostalgic. It is cold, dry, pure, and clear. "It is a simple, strict, one might say puritanical drink," he writes. "Its
pleasure, which is not voluptuous but astringent, can only be
expressed by oxymoron—sensuous coldness, opulent dryness,
mysterious clarity, alluring purity." This is the martini that
Hemingway's Frederic Henry responds to in *A Farewell to
Arms*, when he says, after drinking several, "I had never tasted
anything so cool and clean. They made me feel civilized."
They are the liquid counterpart of Hemingway's prose.

It could also be argued that the martini is capitalist. It is the official drink of America's business class, the high-octane fuel that powered Wall Street and Madison Avenue well into the 1970s, when the age of Perrier and lime began. It's tempting to argue that these professions, involving more than the usual moral compromises required of adult life, find renewal in the martini, whose clarity and purity represent the uncorrupted soul of the corrupt man, just as the preppy look pays homage to his youthful idealism and physical grace. In a world built on equivocation, the businessman can insist with utter fanaticism on the martini as he likes it, *demands* it: drier than dry.

The dry martini is a virtuous martini. Vermouth carries with it the sense of taint, and its rejection is an essential part of the modern martini ritual. Paradoxically, it is never more present than when it is totally absent. "The affliction that is cutting down the productive time in the office and destroying the benign temper of most bartenders is the thing called the *very* dry martini," the *New York Times* complained in 1952. "It's a mass madness, a cult, a frenzy, a body of folklore, a mystique, an *expertise* of a sort which may very well earn for this decade the name of the Numb (or Glazed) 50's."

The *Times* account noted that at one midtown bar, martinis were being listed as dry, very dry, and extra dry, with an additional dime tacked onto the price at each step. There is no reason why three or four even drier categories could not have been created, since, past a certain point, dryness becomes a notion rather than an actual taste sensation. Many a bartender has served up an icy glass of pure gin, only to have it returned with the angry demand, "Make it again, but dry this time." Schenley Distillers once tried to capitalize on the trend by launching a product called the Naked Martini, designed to be stored in the freezer and poured straight into a glass. It was pure gin, cut to 80 proof, the idea being that this would approximate the taste of a no-vermouth martini slightly diluted by ice cubes.

Martini lore abounds in fanciful ways of rejecting vermouth. It's enough to show the vermouth label to the martini glass, or to whisper "vermouth" while shaking the drink. In the *Thin Man* films, actor William Powell used a medicine dropper to dispense the vermouth. Truth imitated fiction when a company began selling a vermouth atomizer. Progress continues in this area: the serious martini drinker can now order vermouth-soaked olives from a mail-order catalog.

No religion can exist without heresy, and the martini has witnessed its share. In 1951, a Chicago liquor dealer held a contest for variations on the martini and received two hundred entries. The twenty-five finalists included martinis made with sauternes, Scotch, and liebfraumilch. There was a martini that called for a slice of garlic to be rubbed around the rim of the glass. The winner was a martini served in a glass rinsed with Cointreau and garnished with an anchovy-stuffed olive. In 1959, a Washington, D.C., bar achieved momentary fame by promoting the "dillytini," a martini containing a string bean that had been marinated in dill vinegar. The same year, a Chicago restaurateur by the name of Morton C. Morton triumphantly announced the invention of the Mortini: gin, vermouth, and a peeled bermuda onion. The drink, Morton said, was enjoyed "only by people with the most fashionable psychoses."

For a time, from the late 1960s through the 1970s, the martini went into steep decline. Younger drinkers did not seem to be replenishing the ranks. The martini was their father's drink, and they didn't want it any more than they wanted Dad's music or hairstyle. "Young people do not like martinis and they're not drinking them. Ever! Anywhere!" James Villas wrote in *Esquire* in 1973, assessing the martini mood. "It stands for everything from phony bourgeois values and social snobbery to jaded alcoholism and latent masochism."

Because young people were not drinking martinis, nervous trend watchers assumed that the drink was dead. But Villas conducted a little experiment. He sat down in the Oak Bar at the Plaza Hotel and watched its two bartenders at work. They served about five hundred cocktails during the afternoon rush. About three hundred were martinis, drunk by men over thirty. Demographics were on the martini's side. As the baby boom aged and prospered, it would find its way back to the martini.

It took a while. As late as 1985, *Time* could call the martini an "amusing antique." No more. As the century drew to a close, the martini returned with a vengeance, riding on a wave of nostalgia for the cocktail era of the 1920s, Hollywood films of the glamour age, and even the swinging Rat Pack ethos of Dean and Frank and Sammy. Fashionable restaurants in the 1990s began serving tuna tartare in martini glasses. Strange apparitions like the watermelon martini evolved into even stranger drinks like the Snickertini (sweet liqueurs mixed with vanilla ice cream and garnished with cubes of candy bar). A bar in Washington, D.C., served a sake martini garnished with a baby octopus.

The obsession is not hard to understand. Despite its nineteenth-century origins, the martini has become fixed in the popular imagination as a deco drink. It harks back to the surge of optimistic modernism when the bold, clean lines of the Bauhaus and de Stijl and the new ideas of industrial design set pulses racing. The classic martini glass, a simple, minimalist geometric form, ranks as one of the era's enduring legacies. As an image, a cultural icon, and a fashion accessory, it exudes an almost seductive allure.

Something strange yet perhaps predictable happened to the

martini as it cruised toward the twenty-first century. Vodka supplanted gin. The "purer" vodka now goes into two out of every three martinis. The logic of the martini has turned the drink inside out. It now glows in perfect transparency—sans vermouth, sans botanicals, sans everything.

It is pleasing to think that the first Americans, adherents of a fierce, uncompromising faith, would recognize the vodka martini as their own. It is a Puritan drink, and it is to the Puritans that we now turn, the intolerant creators of a free and tolerant society, enemies of frivolity who laid the foundations for that most frivolous of American creations, the cocktail.

TWO

CONCEIVED IN LIBERTY

If barley be wanting to make into malt,
We must be content and think it no fault,
For we can make liquor to sweeten our lips,
Of pumpkins, and parsnips, and walnut-tree chips.
—Anonymous, 1630s

The Puritans arrived on the shores of New England with a passion for freedom and a raging thirst. When the Pilgrims dropped anchor at Plymouth Rock, it was no coincidence that the liquor supply was getting low. William Bradford, anxiously scanning the rocky shoreline of Massachusetts, decided not to "take time for further search or consideration, our victuals being much spent, especially our Beere." This was no joking matter. The *Mayflower* had brought along a cooper for the express purpose of tending the precious kegs: none other than John Alden, who later found gainful employment in Longfellow's *Courtship of Miles Standish*.

The early settlers thought long and hard about securing adequate supplies of liquid refreshment before leaving the old country. When John Winthrop, the first governor of the Massachusetts Bay Colony, set sail to America on the *Arabella*, his stores included 10,000 gallons of beer, 120 hogsheads of malt for brewing, and 12 gallons of "hot waters," or ardent spirits. That was the official supply. Just in case, most families brought their own backup barrels.

The colonists, to put it mildly, were no teetotalers. The word did not even exist until the temperance movement of the early nineteenth century. The concept didn't exist either. In their war on sensory pleasure, the Puritans never considered attacking beer and wine as inherently harmful. Intoxication was sinful, of course, and Increase Mather denounced excessive toasting in *Wo to Drunkards* (1673). But no one condemned alcohol outright. Drink was a gift of God, a source of good cheer, the seal of friendship. Even more, it was a kind of food, a sustaining and strength-giving substance. No worker was expected to toil throughout the day without alcoholic fortification.

Water was the liquid of last resort. It carried disease, and the colonists regarded the gurgling streams of the New World with a suspicious eye. Although William Wood of the Massachusetts Bay Colony gave high marks to the American product, finding it to be "not so sharp, but of a fatter substance, and of a more jetty color" than English water, he still balked. "I dare not prefer it before good Beere, as some have done," he wrote. For the colonists, it was imperative to ensure a steady supply of good drink.

The obstacles were formidable. European vines failed to take on American soil, and the Eastern Seaboard was ill-suited to the grain needed to brew beer or distill alcohol. As a result, wine and brandy, as well as most beer and porter—beer's richer, darker cousin—had to be imported. In Boston, ships

laden with fish and barrel staves set sail for the Canaries and
Azores, where casks were banged together and filled up with
wine for the return journey. The cod-for-wine business flourished, so much so that as early as 1645 the Massachusetts General Court found it worthwhile to establish duties on madeira
and sherry, as well as such now-forgotten favorites as bastard (a
sweet Spanish wine made from the bastardo grape), malaga (a
sweet fortified wine made in Andalusia), canary (the now-
extinct sherry of the Canary Islands), tent (from the Spanish
tinto, or red), and alicante (a robust red from Spain's Mediter-
ranean coast).

Madeira was far and away the favorite wine of the colonies,
in part because it actually improved with travel, but also because it was relatively cheap. The Navigation Acts required
that all European goods transported to America be carried on
English ships, an expensive proposition. But the island of
Madeira, a Portuguese possession, was geographically part of
Africa, so its wines could be shipped direct. That made them a
bargain, and wildly popular—a quarter of the island's total
production went to North America—until a devastating fun-
gus virtually wiped out Madeira's vines in the middle of the
nineteenth century. When the Founding Fathers proposed a
toast after signing the Declaration of Independence, it was
madeira they reached for. So pronounced was the taste for
madeira that as late as the 1830s the Astor House in Manhattan offered forty-two varieties on its wine list.

Ever alert for new ways to squeeze money out of the
colonies, the British clamped down with the Revenue Act of
1764, imposing stiff duties on wines from Madeira and the
Azores and low duties on Spanish and Portuguese wines. The
idea was to encourage consumption of port, whose trade went
through Britain, and to fatten the British treasury. If the

colonists insisted on drinking madeira, fine. Let them pay for it. The British would win either way.

But the Americans did not cooperate. The more idealistic organized a boycott of taxed goods, with Yale College in the vanguard. This early example of campus radicalism was cheered on by patriots. "All Gentlemen of Taste, who visit the College," the *New York Gazette* wrote, "will think themselves better entertained with a good glass of Beer or Cider, offered them upon such principles, that they could be with the best Punch or Madeira." The more practical solution was smuggling, and at this the colonists were past masters. In one official report to the Customs Board, it was noted that thirty vessels arriving in New York from Madeira and the Azores did not declare enough goods to fill even one ship. Even the dimmest-witted customs clerk could account for the difference.

After madeira, the most popular wines were canary, port, sherry, malaga, and fayal (from the island of the same name in the Azores). French wines, especially from Bordeaux, could be found on the best tables, most notably Thomas Jefferson's, where guests could enjoy not only the best of Bordeaux, Burgundy, and Champagne, but southern French wines from Roussillon, Provence, Frontignan, and Limoux; sauternes from the fabled Chateau d'Yquem; and, most unusual, Montepulciano wines from Italy. According to his slave Isaac, Jefferson also kept on hand some fine twelve-year-old rum from Antigua.

Imports were fine for the gentry, but they could not possibly satisfy popular demand. For that, the colonists would have to develop their own resources, and they set about the task with a will. By 1629, Virginia had two brewhouses. Boston established its first malt house in 1637. On Staten Island, grain (probably corn or rye) was distilled into alcohol in 1640 by

Willem Kieft, director general of the colony of New Nether-land. Mead and metheglin, fermented from honey, were made throughout the colonies.

On a small scale, the colonies tried to reproduce the drinks of the Old World. Very soon, though, the need to improvise be-came apparent. Since ingredients for the traditional beverages were not always available, whatever grew locally was pressed into service. Showing the can-do spirit that would pull Amer-ica through Prohibition, the colonial farmer turned to any-thing that would ferment. St. John de Crèvecoeur, in his "Journey into Northern Pennsylvania and the State of New York," reported that ingenious farmers were making beer from pine chips, pine buds, hemlock, fir needles, roasted corn, dried apple skins, sassafras roots, and bran. He could have added parsnips, currants, and elderberries as well. In Virginia, accord-ing to Governor William Berkeley, "the poorer sort brew their beer with molasses and bran: with indian corn malted with drying in a stove; with persimmons dried in a cake and baked; with potatoes with the green stalks of Indian corn cut small and bruised, with pompions [pumpkins]." Last and least es-teemed for brewing beer was the Jerusalem artichoke.

Spruce beer, made by adding spruce twigs to malt for extra flavor, formed part of the soldier's ration. Governor John Winthrop, Jr., of Connecticut brewed beer from corn, an achievement that won him election to the Royal Society of London. Peaches and pears were used to make ciders, known as peachy and perry. Peaches were also distilled into brandy, espe-cially in the South.

Wherever apples grew (English seed had been introduced to America by 1630), cider became popular, eclipsing beer in New England by the middle of the seventeenth century. John Josselyn, who left records of two voyages to New England, in

1638 and 1663, enjoyed cider spiced and sweetened with sugar in Boston's taphouses. He also recommended the following embellished version: "Take of Malago-Raisins, stamp them and put milk to them in a Hippocras bag and let it drain out of itself, put a quantity of this with a spoonful or two of Syrup of Clove-Gilliflowers into every bottle when you bottle your Cyder." (Hippocras, a spiced wine passed through a muslin sleeve, was a medieval favorite, mentioned by Chaucer in "The Merchant's Tale"; for reasons unknown, its invention was attributed to Hippocrates.)

Cider, the farmer's joy, became synonymous with good, honest living and a lack of pretense. Cheaper than beer, it was served to children and to college students. It was drunk morning, noon, and night. John Adams enjoyed a full tankard before breakfast every morning. In the 1840 presidential campaign, cider even became a political issue. The Democratic candidate, Martin Van Buren, was painted by the Whigs as a sissified drinker of wines, up to and including champagne, while William Henry Harrison was marketed to the voters as a humble son of the soil, born in a log cabin and best pleased with the rustic life. One campaign song went:

> Let Van from his coolers of silver drink wine,
> And lounge on his cushioned settee;
> Our man on his buckeye bench can recline,
> Content with hard cider is he.

The Whigs sounded this theme loud and often—so much so that a New Hampshire Democrat, recalling the campaign, remarked dryly, "No Whig gentleman considered himself properly adorned with the ensigns of his party, unless he carried a cane with a miniature hard cider barrel for its head, or an umbrella similarly adorned."

For a more potent drink, New Englanders put their cider outdoors in cold weather, waited for it to freeze, and then skimmed off the ice. An improvement on this rough-and-ready method came in 1698, when a Scottish distiller named William Laird settled in Monmouth County, New Jersey, and began making apple brandy, or applejack. (The commercial distillery founded a century later by one of his descendants, Laird & Co. of Scobeyville, today makes more than 95 percent of the applejack in the United States.) By the 1830s, nearly four hundred distilleries in New Jersey were producing "Jersey lightning," enjoyed straight or in such winter warmers as scotchem, a mixture of applejack, boiling water, and a dab of mustard.

The preeminent spirit of the colonies, however, was rum. Columbus had brought sugarcane cuttings to Hispaniola on his second voyage, in 1493. The plant thrived, and it did not take long for planters to discover a use for the cane left over after the sugar was extracted from it. In 1651, an anonymous account of Barbados noted that "the chief fudling they make in the island is Rumbullion, alias Kill-Devil, and this is made of sugar cane distilled, a hot, hellish, and terrible liquor."

Soon the colonies began trading with the West Indies, and the reign of rum began. Almost from the outset, it developed a sinister reputation. For generations, historians argued that rum formed one side of the "triangle trade" between America, the West Indies, and Africa. Slaves from Africa were exchanged in the West Indies for molasses, which was brought to New England and distilled into rum. New England ships would then transport rum to West Africa and trade it for slaves, who worked the sugarcane fields that yielded the molasses. More recent scholarship has shown the triangle trade to be myth, not fact. The slave trade never counted for much in New England's economy. But rum did. By 1763, New England had 159 rum distilleries. Boston alone had thirty, and nearly a thousand sailing vessels traded in rum out of the city. From Philadelphia northward, distillation of rum was the leading manufacturing process.

So many of New England's distilleries were clustered around Medford, about six miles northeast of Boston, that "Medford rum" became a kind of generic term—a much more plausible one than the slang word "stinkibus." Although it is true that before his famous ride, Paul Revere took refuge in the home of Isaac Hall, captain of the Medford Minute Men and a distiller, there is no reason to believe the legend that he downed a few quick ones for the road.

Much of the drinking in early America took place in public houses. The colonial tavern, originally known as an "ordinary," was hotel, saloon, and municipal building all in one. To the traveler, it offered room and board. In the days before courthouses and town halls, it gave public officials a place to conduct business, with the town's freemen footing the bill. Mail was delivered and distributed at the tavern, and on militia days, court days, and election days, its open doors beckoned. When rebellion began to simmer in the colonies, strategy sessions were held over a tankard at the local. It did not take long for the tavern to rival the church as a social institution. The home of good cheer and warming drinks, it provided fellowship and entertainment, even gambling. Billiards and bowling were on offer, as well as shuffleboard and cards. In the South, cockfighting and bullbaiting pulled in the crowds. Traveling players often used the tavern as a rehearsal hall. Auctions were held at taverns, and dances too.

The tavern was the natural showcase for acrobats, conjurers, and curiosities of every sort. Exotic beasts could always be counted on to draw a crowd hungry for self-improvement. One advertisement offered: "A *beautiful* MOOSE. The curious in natural history are invited to Major King's Tavern, where it is to be seen a fine young moose of 16 hands in height, and well-proportioned. The properties of this fleet and tractable animal are such as will give pleasure and satisfaction to every beholder." Polar bears and performing apes also went on tour. And who could resist the "Female Sampson," who lay prone between two chairs, supporting a 300-pound anvil that two men struck with sledgehammers?

A forum for political debate, the tavern offered mental stimulation as well, and on occasion it hosted formal battles of wit. In 1756, two contestants in Massachusetts, Jonathan Gower of Lynn and Joseph Emerson of Reading, met by arrangement at a local tavern to engage in intellectual struggle. History, alas, has left no record of the verbal cut and thrust. We know only that Gower retired in defeat, vanquished by Emerson, whose wit, according to one spectator, "was beyond all human imagination."

The tone was not always so elevated. Perhaps more typical was the experience of Sarah Knight, a Boston teacher who sampled a number of inns and taverns on her journey from Boston to New York in 1704. Her journal challenges the image of the colonial tavern as an American agora in which freedom-loving citizens discoursed on the rights of man. In a Dedham tavern, seeking a guide for her journey, Knight asked the hostess to canvass the room. She received no response, as the men were "tyed by the Lipps" to their tankards. At a tavern in Rhode Island, she was kept up all night by two men arguing over the origin of "Narragansett."

The main attraction at any tavern, of course, was the refreshment, and here the native genius showed itself in full splendor. Every drink invited a dozen variations, every punch

begged for an extra exotic ingredient. The diaries of Benjamin
Lynde, chief justice of the Massachusetts Bay Colony, paint a
striking picture of American-style refreshment in the 1730s
and 1740s. As he traveled from town to town, Lynde enjoyed a
remarkable variety of drinks, from madeira, brandy punch,
lime punch, cider, and ale to "sugar brandy dram," "tankard
bounce," "cherry dram," and a very strange item described as
"sage ale and chocolate."

By temperament, Americans were never content to let well
enough alone. In 1753, Israel Acrelius, a Swedish pastor, com-
piled a list of the drinks he encountered on a tour through the
Delaware Valley. All but three of his forty-eight beverages
were alcoholic, beginning with French wine and proceeding
through four kinds of cider and nearly twenty rum drinks (including punch, sling, and grog) to sangaree, syllabub, and
mead. American beer he pronounced "brown, thick, and un-
palatable."

Most of these drinks have gone the way of the pewter mug
and the powdered wig. Cider royal, according to Acrelius, came
in two versions. In the first, brandy was added to a barrel of
cider along with several pounds of muscovado (cane) sugar,

Poor Mug, unfortunate is thy Condition! Of thy self thou wouldst do no
Harm, but much Harm is done with thee! Thou art accused of many Mis-
chiefs; thou art said to administer Drunkenness, Poison, and broken
Heads: But none praise thee for the good Things thou yieldest! Shouldest
thou produce double Beer, nappy Ale, stallcop Cyder, or Cyder mull'd,
fine Punch, or cordial Tiff; yet for all these shouldst thou not be prais'd,
but the rich Liquors themselves, which tho' within thee, twill be said to be
foreign to thee!
—Benjamin Franklin, "A Meditation on a Quart Mug" (1733)

which boosted the alcohol content and added flavor. If the ingredients were left to sit for a year, or sent on a sea voyage, the result was called apple wine. The second version of cider royal called for equal parts cider and mead to be fermented together.

Syllabub, now a kind of dessert, loomed large in colonial drinking. A nineteenth-century article on the colonial tavern gives two recipes. The first: "Fill your syllabub pot with cider, and a good store of sugar; put in as much thick cream by two or three spoonfulls at a time, as hard as you can, as though you milk it, then stir it together exceedingly softly over and about and let it stand two hours at least." The second: "Take the juice and grated outer skin of a large lemon, four glasses of cider, ¼ pound sifted sugar, mix, let stand some hours, then whip it and add a pint of thick cream and the whites of two eggs cut to a froth." In her *American Cookery* (1796), Amelia Simmons takes a no-nonsense approach: "Sweeten a quart of cider with double refined sugar, grate nutmeg into it, then milk your cow into your liquor." The nineteenth century would have been scandalized to see the word "liquor" in a work meant for the family kitchen, but in colonial America, punches and syllabubs were simply part of the cuisine.

Many tavern menus offered sangaree, a corruption of the Spanish *sangría*. It was made by diluting red wine with water and lemon juice, then adding grated nutmeg and sometimes sugar. Madeira was the favored base wine, later supplanted by port and sherry. Sack-posset, a favorite at weddings and feasts, was ale and sherry thickened with eggs and cream, then seasoned with nutmeg, mace, and sugar, and boiled for two hours over a fire. Negus, named after a British colonel of the same name, was port or claret heated, sweetened with sugar, and flavored with lemon and grated nutmeg.

Not every tavern served all forty-eight of the drinks on

Acrelius's list, but most had a beverage menu of baroque complexity compared to the shot-and-a-beer joint of the present day. A typical bill of fare, from a New York tavern in 1790, offered "good madeira wine" by the pint, other foreign wines, "fruit punch of good spirits and loaf sugar" in quart bowls, mulled cider, "egg or other sling, with a gill of West India rum in it and loaf sugar," West India rum, cherry rum, gin, brandy, cider royal, metheglin, "good double beer," and "good cyder." Gin, it should be noted, is but one of many offerings. In America it never attained anything like the popularity it enjoyed in England, where it was the universal tipple of the urban poor.

Nor did Acrelius exhaust the rum repertoire, even with nearly twenty drinks. The plain man's approach was to mix rum with a little water. Half and half made a sling. One part rum and three parts water was grog. Calibogus, or bogus, was cold rum and beer, unsweetened. Rum and cherry juice made cherry bounce. Bombo or bumbo was rum, sugar, water, and nutmeg; without the nutmeg, it became mimbo. Rum mixed with molasses was black-strap, and country stores served it out of the barrel, which had a dried salted cod dangling alongside it, a free snack that usually encouraged extra orders, like the salted nuts of today's bars.

Festive occasions inspired more fanciful rum drinks. Flip, which appeared around 1690, was beer sweetened with sugar, molasses, or dried pumpkin and strengthened with rum. A red-hot iron was thrust into the mixture, causing it to foam and take on a burnt, bitter flavor. The iron was known as a hottle, a flip dog, or a loggerhead, whose use as a weapon gave rise to the expression "to be at loggerheads."

Recipes for flip varied, but the following, from Abbott's Tavern in Massachusetts, is typical:

Keep grated ginger and nutmeg with a fine dried lemon peel rubbed together in a mortar. To make a quart of flip put the ale on the fire to warm, and beat up three or four eggs with four ounces of moist sugar, a teaspoon of grated nutmeg or ginger, and a quartern of good old rum or brandy. When the ale is near to boil, put into one pitcher, and the rum and eggs, etc., into another: turn it from one pitcher into another until it is as smooth as cream. To heat, plunge in the red-hot loggerhead or poker. This quantity is styled one yard of flannel.

The pride of most taverns, and a centerpiece of festive occasions, was rum punch, flavored with shrub, lemon, or orange juice. Well into the nineteenth century, punch dominated whenever liquors were mixed. The most famous was Fish House Punch, the official drink of an eccentric social club— the peculiarly named State in Schuylkill—founded near Philadelphia in 1732 and still in existence. Its thirty members, or "governors," would periodically head out to the club's headquarters, a wooden castle on the Schuylkill River known as the Fish House, where they would don white aprons, fry perch on outdoor barbecue grills, and drink punch.

Legend credits a Captain Samuel Morris with inventing the punch, although one club member who looked into the matter decided that the recipe came straight from a seventeenth-century punch favored by the Farmers' Club in London. Recipes for Fish House Punch abound, nearly all of them spurious. Dr. William Camac, a governor of the State in Schuylkill, recorded the official one in 1873. It calls for one quart each of lemon juice and brandy, two quarts of rum, five pounds of sugar, and nine pounds of water and ice (four and a half quarts). It's a simple, even banal punch, and how it developed such a mystique remains unclear.

Foreign visitors found all this mixing and stirring a bit much, not to mention the nomenclature. John Bernard, an English comic actor who toured the United States from 1797 to 1811, observed with some amusement the daily schedule of a Virginia plantation owner, who started the day with a "mint sling" at 9 a.m. and then, after a brief tour of his estate, settled into a day of serious drinking. Bernard did not know quite what to make of what he saw. "Between twelve and one," he wrote, "his throat would require another emulsion, and he would sip half a pint of some mystery termed bumbo, apple-toddy, or pumpkin flip."

The American flair for improvisation and uninhibited mixing appeared early on, but the historian searches in vain for the proto-martini or an Ur-Manhattan. Most drinks were hot, a legacy of the British drink culture, in which the first duty of an alcoholic beverage was to ward off the chill. The colonists, as though unaware of America's blazing hot summers, continued to favor drinks designed to stoke the internal stove. Ice, of course, was a luxury. But prevailing notions of physiology would have favored the consumption of hot drinks in any case, and in any weather. Sweat drew heat from the body, and as a result, wrote one early chronicler, "the inner parts are left cold and faint."

The great ice age of drink lay in the future. The early Americans could do no more than clear the ground and plant the seeds that would yield a harvest for future generations. Their lasting contribution is the spirit of experiment and improvisation in matters of drink, still the great divide between the New and Old Worlds when it comes to mixing a cocktail. By breaking with tradition and throwing off the dead hand of the past, they prepared the way for the cocktail's triumph.

{THREE}

FIRST STIRRINGS

The cordial drop, the morning dram, I sing,
The mid-day toddy, and the evening sling.
—*The Massachusetts Spy*, July 16, 1806

As America picked up and headed west, it left rum behind and perfected the art of whiskey-making. This was a giant step in the cocktail's evolution, for it was whiskey—first rye, then bourbon—that predominated in the first recognizably modern mixed drinks: the mint julep and the whiskey-and-bitters drink known as a bittered sling.

Whiskey was not entirely unknown to the colonists. At Jamestown in the early years of the seventeenth century, Captain George Thorpe distilled liquor from maize and dashed off an excited letter to London. "I have found a way to make so good a drink of Indian corn," he wrote, "as I protest I have divers times refused to drink good strong English beer and chosen to drink that." When Governor Alexander Spotswood of Virginia led his "Knights of the Golden Horseshoe" across the Blue Ridge Mountains in 1716, hoping to find the Indian

Ocean on the other side, his provisions included not only red and white wine from Virginia, brandy, shrub, rum, champagne, canary, punch, and cider, but also an unspecified quantity of "Irish usquebaugh," or whiskey.

But virtually no whiskey was distilled before the Revolution. Israel Acrelius, writing in the 1750s, reported that it was drunk "far up in the interior of the country, where rum is very dear on account of the transportation." Elsewhere, hard-to-grow grain made whiskey prohibitively expensive in comparison with rum. During the Revolutionary War, however, when neither rum nor molasses could be imported from the British West Indies, demand for spirits leaped, as thousands of men enlisted as soldiers. Suddenly, it became immensely profitable to distill rye and even wheat into whiskey, and the Scotch-Irish who began arriving in America in the 1730s knew how to do it. The entrepreneurial response to demand was so enthusiastic, in fact, that for a time it threatened the bread supply.

After the war, the pioneers who pushed across western Maryland and Pennsylvania soon found that it was cost-effective to distill rye into whiskey and ship it back east in barrels. A packhorse could carry only four bushels of grain, but it could haul the equivalent of twenty-four bushels distilled into two kegs of whiskey. Soon there were five thousand log stillhouses in the frontier counties of Fayette, Allegheny, Westmoreland, and Washington, turning out the dry, piquant whiskey that would make the name Monongahela synonymous with quality.

By 1788, a traveler reporting to the *Philadelphia Museum*, a newspaper, stated that "in the neighborhood of Pittsburgh almost every other farm has a stillhouse on it. . . . All the rye in those parts is distilled into whiskey, and wheat is often given in exchange for it. Plantations are often bought and sold for a certain number of barrels of whiskey. Indeed, whiskey in different quantities, like Montero's cap in *Tristram Shandy*, is the wager, the gift, and in some instances, the oath of three-fourths of the inhabitants of our western counties." The whiskey habit had spread to the German farmers of Lancaster and Berks counties, who, he noted with astonishment, poured the liquor over cucumbers at breakfast. The traveler may have been confused. François André Michaux, a Frenchman who toured the western frontier in 1805, reported that the local inhabitants soaked the green cones of the so-called cucumber tree (actually a kind of magnolia) in whiskey to create a bitters that was thought to ward off fever.

Either way, whiskey quickly became integrated into the fabric of daily life. George Washington himself went into the whiskey business. His last estate manager at Mount Vernon was a Scot named James Anderson, who persuaded Washington to start growing rye for whiskey on one of his unprofitable small farms. Soon Washington had a thriving operation that turned a profit of £83 in 1798, producing not only whiskey but apple, peach, and persimmon brandy. Jefferson, too, had a rye distillery.

It is a little ironic, then, that the distillation of whiskey should have led to the first test of federal power, after the government introduced an excise tax on spirits in 1791 to help pay off war debts. The cash-poor farmers of western Pennsylvania refused to pay. Then they began harassing tax collectors. Finally, they mounted a revolt. In August 1794, Washington sent in federal troops, about thirteen thousand of them. That settled the argument.

But the disgruntled farmers of the Whiskey Rebellion simply pushed west into Kentucky, and there, where corn grew abundantly, they invented America's most enduring gift to the world of spirits: bourbon whiskey.

Just who can lay claim to the invention of bourbon remains

unclear. George Thorpe, back in Jamestown, distilled a kind of whiskey from corn, which entitles him to a footnote in bourbon history, but modern bourbon is a far different product, distilled from corn, a small percentage of rye or wheat, and malted barley, and aged in charred new oak barrels. The result is a plump, fruity, russet-colored whiskey. Its evolution is mysterious, shrouded in myth, self-interested claims, and folk history.

We know that distilling took place on the western frontier even before the Whiskey Rebellion. Corn and rye were grown in Kentucky during the Revolution, and scattered references suggest that stills were operating in the 1770s and 1780s. In 1789, Representative George Thatcher of Massachusetts ridiculed the "new-fangled distillates produced in other states," made from such raw ingredients as rye, apples, and peaches.

In 1776, Elijah Pepper settled near Lexington, Kentucky, and reportedly set up a still around 1780. The family firm, which flourished under Elijah's grandson James E. Pepper, produced a whiskey called Old 1776, whose slogan, "Born with the Republic," may have been exaggerated, but only slightly. Another perennial candidate in the bourbon sweepstakes is Evan Williams, officially registered as the first man to open a distillery in Kentucky, in 1783.

Traditionally, credit for inventing Kentucky bourbon has gone to Elijah Craig, a Baptist preacher who supposedly turned out the first true bourbon in 1789 in Scott County. Gerald Carson, in *The Social History of Bourbon*, calls the Craig claim history, if history is "fiction agreed upon." Henry G. Crowgey, in his scholarly *Kentucky Bourbon*, writes reasonably that "what actually happened was that a people moved in who regarded liquor as a necessity of life." And in the same mysteri-

ous way that the folk music of Ireland evolved into the hill-
billy music of Appalachia, its whiskey became bourbon.

Initially, the "new-fangled distillate" was known simply as
whiskey, but gradually it became obvious that Kentucky was
turning out a distinctive product—full-bodied, mellow, and
smooth. By the early nineteenth century, "Kentucky whiskey"
and "Western whiskey" were recognized trade terms. The
term "Bourbon whiskey" appeared in 1821. But "Bourbon"
might simply have indicated the place of origin rather than a
style: the original Bourbon County embraced all or much
of present-day Kentucky's thirty-four counties, so Kentucky
whiskey and Bourbon whiskey were more or less synonymous.
As the century wore on, the term "Old Bourbon" came into
use. Today, straight bourbon whiskey refers to a spirit made
from a mash of no less than 51 percent corn and aged at least
two years in new white-oak barrels that have been charred on
the inside. (If the grain content is 51 percent rye, the result is
rye whiskey.)

But was the whiskey really bourbon? Unlike true bourbon,
the early-nineteenth-century product was colorless, and the
charring of casks (probably an effort to remove unwanted flavors
from old casks that had been used for nonwhiskey purposes, or to
burn off the splinters and blisters in new casks) seems to have
developed only gradually. In *The Book of Bourbon and Other
Fine American Whiskeys*, Gary Regan and Mary Haidin Regan
propose that between 1800 and 1840 Kentucky's distillers, feeling their way along, began to notice that charring lent smoothness, as well as a distinctive reddish tinge, to their whiskey.

Whatever its origins, bourbon eventually became associated
with one of the earliest and greatest of American cocktails, the
mint julep. The word comes from the Arabic *julab*, or rosewa-
ter, and can be found in Milton, but in its modern meaning it

first surfaces in 1787. A Virginian of the lower or middle class, wrote an early traveler, "rises in the morning, about six o'clock. He then drinks a julap, made of rum, water, and sugar, but very strong." Clearly, this is not the julep of song and story, but a precursor. The first reference to mint comes in 1803, when John Davis, an Englishman employed as a tutor on a Virginia plantation, explained that a julep was "a dram of spirituous liquor that has mint in it, taken by Virginians of a morning." Evidently, news of the julep was slow to travel north, since Webster, in 1806, defines it as "a kind of liquid medicine."

Frederick Marryat, an English naval officer and novelist who toured the United States in the 1830s, was so fascinated by the julep that he recorded, in admirable detail, the full recipe:

> Put into a tumbler about a dozen tender shoots of mint, upon them put a spoonful of white sugar, and equal proportions of peach and common brandy, so as to fill up one third, or perhaps a little less. Then take rasped or pounded ice, and fill up the tumbler. Epicures rub the lip of the tumbler with a piece of fresh pineapple, and the tumbler itself is very often encrusted outside with stalactites of ice. As the ice melts, you drink.

The lavish use of ice marks the julep as an upper-class drink. Before commercial ice harvesting began in the mid-nineteenth century, only substantial estates or hotels maintained icehouses.

The julep appears to have been a popular everyday drink, the Coca-Cola of its time. Basil Hall, yet another of the many English travelers who crossed the Atlantic to observe America in the making, reported that during a seventeen-hour journey in Virginia in the late 1820s his stagecoach stopped at ten public houses. At each stop, his companions alighted to drink a mint julep. Hall expressed amazement that, except for a slight slurring of the speech and an increasing earnestness in their discussions, his fellow travelers seemed none the worse for wear at the end of the trip.

In his treatise on the mint julep, Richard Barksdale Harwell locates the julep's origins in the northern Virginia tidewater country, whence it traveled to Maryland and eventually to Kentucky. At first, the drink was made with the local whiskey, rye. But by the 1830s, the drink more or less conformed to Marryat's recipe. The well-to-do used brandy; others settled for whiskey. After the Civil War, with the South impoverished, brandy disappeared altogether, and the bourbon mint julep became universal.

Harwell is not exactly an unprejudiced witness. His pamphlet, published by the University Press of Virginia, is dedicated to the proposition that the julep can only be Virginian—nay, that bourbon itself is Virginian, since what is now Kentucky formed part of Virginia until 1792. That includes Bourbon County.

In pressing Virginia's claims, Harwell keeps alive a controversy that has been raging for decades. In truth, the wrangling is tedious, carried on in ponderously "humorous" editorials. On occasion a Virginia newspaper will decide to antagonize Kentucky by asserting once more that bourbon, and therefore the julep, originated in the Old Dominion State. Usually this occurs around Kentucky Derby time. The joke lies in Kentucky's being seen as a kind of shabby, downmarket version of Virginia. Kentucky, for its part, considers Virginia snooty and stuck-up. "We have lived to see the Emperor of Japan confess that he is not a god," the *Louisville Courier-Journal* wrote in a 1946 julep-inspired tirade, "but we do not expect to live to hear a Virginian say Virginians are no better than other people."

If the mark of a great cocktail is the number of arguments it can provoke, and the number of unbreakable rules it generates, then the mint julep may be America's preeminent classic, edging out the martini in a photo finish. When weary of the Virginia-Kentucky debate, julep fanciers can filibuster for days on the mint issue: whether 'tis nobler to bruise or to crush. When tired of bickering over mint leaves, julep pedants can address another vexed issue: Should the drink be sipped from the glass or through a straw? This point of contention, perpetually on the simmer, boiled over on a slow news day, when the *Courier-Journal* decided to lay down the law. Straws are mandatory, it declared, to keep one's face out of the mint shrubbery.

Kentucky has only to speak, and Virginia strikes back. The *Richmond Times-Dispatch* responded that straws are fit only for lemonade and sarsaparilla, adding for good measure, "Juleps aren't worth drinking, when consumed in the Kentucky manner." Less crucial but nevertheless stimulating points of dispute concern ice (cubes, shaved, cracked, or fine powder), sugar (liquid or granulated), drinking vessel (glass or silver), type of bourbon (straight or blend), and so on, ad infinitum.

If there can be any such thing as the official julep recipe, the honors must go to the statesman Henry Clay. By birth a Virginian, he represented Kentucky for more than half a century in the House and Senate. He mixed his juleps thus:

Mint leaves, fresh and tender, should be pressed against a coin-silver goblet and the back of a silver spoon. Only bruise the leaves gently and then remove from the goblet. Half fill with cracked ice. Mellow Bourbon is poured from the jigger and allowed to slide slowly through the cracked ice. In another receptacle, granulated sugar is slowly mixed into chilled limestone water, then poured on top of the ice. While beads of moisture gather on the burnished exterior of the goblet, garnish the frosted brim with the choicest mint. Then sip.

Clay's instructions are heartfelt, even noble. Rarely does a great political figure pay homage to a great cocktail. But America's most significant julep was drunk far from Bourbon County. The place: Baltimore. The year: 1842. The tipplers: Charles Dickens and Washington Irving. On his first tour of America, Dickens recalled:

> Some unknown admirer of his books and mine sent to the hotel a most enormous mint julep, wreathed in flowers. We sat, one on either side of it, with great solemnity (it filled a respectably-sized round table) but the solemnity was of very short duration. It was quite an enchanted julep, and carried us among innumerable people and places we both knew. The julep held out far into the night, and my memory never saw him afterwards otherwise than as bending over it, with his straw, with an attempted air of gravity (after some anecdote involving some wonderfully droll and delicate observation of character), and then as his eye caught mine, melting into that captivating laugh of his, which was the brightest and best that I have ever heard.

The julep, alas, scarcely exists today except as a rather strained evocation of the Old South. Thousands are served at

Churchill Downs on the first Saturday in May, Kentucky
Derby day, but the gesture is purely nostalgic. As a living part
of the culture, the julep has gone the way of Rhett, Scarlett,
and hoop skirts. And it has encountered plenty of abuse on the
way down. In the 1920s, the Savoy Hotel in London served a
champagne julep, and the Winter Palace bar in Nice unleashed
a strange mixture involving cognac, yellow Chartreuse, crème
de menthe, and mint leaves rolled in lemon juice and frosted
with powdered sugar. Charles H. Baker, Jr., who roamed the
wide world looking for exotic drinks, found a julep at the
Manila Hotel in the Philippines that used pineapple slices,
four cherries, and a splash of rum along with the bourbon.

The drink reached its nadir in the 1950s, when a shortcut
julep reared its head: a cold shot of bourbon stirred with a peppermint stick. This quickie underscored, in the harshest way,
the julep's central weakness: it was always a slow, complicated
drink, requiring a servant class to make it. Ordering one is tan-
tamount to saying, "Peel me a grape." Today it is little more
than a caricature of Southern leisure. In 1992, the Southern
Focus Poll put a long list of questions about the South to citizens on both sides of the Mason-Dixon Line. One was, "Have
you ever tasted a mint julep?" Seventy percent of the non-
Southerners answered no. And in a shocking betrayal of their
heritage, 73 percent of Southerners said the same. The julep,
in other words, has reached the end of the road. The South
gave it birth, and the South has buried it. R.I.P.

The mixing of whiskey, bitters, and sugar represents a turning
point, as decisive for American drinking habits as the discovery
of three-point perspective was for Renaissance painting. It is
the beginning of the cocktail in modern form. The cardinal
virtues of warmth and nourishment were giving way to an

aesthetic of refreshment and stimulation, just as the communal atmosphere of the tavern was evolving into the less settled patterns of the barroom, and the punch bowl to the individual drink, often idiosyncratic, crafted specifically for each customer.

The radical changes in American taste can be traced in the remarkable explosion of drink terms in the early nineteenth century. The most important is the word "cocktail" itself. On May 13, 1806, subscribers to the *Balance and Columbian Repository*, a newspaper printed in Hudson, New York, were treated to a lively exchange on the letters page.

Sir, I observe in your paper of the 6th inst., in the account of a democratic candidate for a seat in the Legislature, marked under the head of Loss, 25 do., "cocktail." Will you be so obliging as to inform me what is meant by this species of refreshment? . . . I have heard of a "jorum," of "phlegm cutter" and "fog-driver," of "wetting the whistle" and "moistening the clay," of a "fillip," a "spur in the head," "quenching a spark in the throat," of "flip," etc., but never in my life, though I have lived a good many years, did I hear of cocktail before. Is it peculiar to this part of the country? Or is it a late invention? Is the name expressive of the effect which the drink has on a particular part of the body? Or does it signify that the Democrats who make the potion are turned topsy turvy, and have their heads where their tails are?

The editor's answer:

Cocktail is a stimulating liquor, composed of spirits of any kind, sugar, water, and bitters—it is vulgarly called

a bittered sling and is supposed to be an excellent elec-
tioneering potion, inasmuch as it renders the heart stout
and bold, at the same time that it fuddles the head. It is
said also, to be of great use to a Democratic candidate:
because, a person having swallowed a glass of it, is ready
to swallow anything else.

This is the first known reference to the cocktail in English,
although the thing itself, obviously, predated the word. Charles
William Johnson, an Englishman who toured the United
States between 1793 and 1806, told his readers that "the first
craving of an American in the morning, is for ardent spirits,
mixed with sugar, mint, or some other hot herb, and which are
called slings." If his "hot herb" means bitters—an alcoholic
infusion of bitter herbs, leaves, or roots that stimulate the
palate—then he was describing the same "bittered sling" referred to by the editor of the *Balance*. We may recall, also, the
"mint sling" that John Bernard saw in Virginia in 1799.

Early observers seem to agree that the key ingredient defining a cocktail was bitters. When Edward Henry Durrell, visiting New Orleans in the 1840s, expressed puzzlement at the
term "brandy cocktail," an obliging native gave him a quick
tutorial: "Now the difference between a brandy cocktail and a
brandy toddy is this: a brandy toddy is made by adding together a little water, a little sugar, and a great deal of
brandy—mix well and drink. A brandy cocktail is composed
of the same ingredients, with the addition of a shade of
Stoughton's bitters; so that the bitters draw the line of demar-
cation."

The word "cocktail" itself remains one of the most elusive
in the language. Many writers on drink have accepted the colorful legend of Betsy Flanagan, the widow of a Revolutionary

War soldier, who supposedly kept a Westchester tavern frequented by French soldiers (the town is usually given as Four Corners or Elmsford). One day in 1779, the story goes, she plucked a few feathers from the roosters kept by a Tory neighbor, stuck them in a glass, and served them as a garnish for a punch. In a celebratory toast, her customers cried out, "*Vive le cock-tail.*"

Let us examine this thoroughly spurious anecdote, since it bears many of the distinctive features of the fake histories that abound in literature on drink. First, like a bad alibi, it is both too vague and too specific. The idea that a whim of the moment—placing a cock's "tail" in a glass on a particular evening—would generate a new word that passed forever into the American language strains credulity. In addition, the word does not appear in print for another twenty-seven years. In any case, the Franglais of *Vive le cock-tail* is ludicrous.

The Flanagan story is a striking example of what might be called barroom etymology, a pseudodiscipline that bears the same relation to real etymology that barroom argument does to the thought of Kant or Hegel. It rests on the wobbly premise that each and every cocktail was invented on a specific occasion by a particular bartender, who looked on his new drink, cried *Eureka!,* and gave it a fanciful name. Because this notion has a grip on the popular mind, nearly every drink comes fitted out with a preposterous origin story, concocted according to the following rules: spin a yarn, embellish it, and then throw in a few gaudy details to give it an authentic feel, while remaining vague on the main points. Buff and polish it in the retelling. After three repetitions, present it as historical fact.

Who was Betsy Flanagan, exactly? She first surfaces in a work of fiction, James Fenimore Cooper's *The Spy*, published in 1821 but set in the 1780s. Often described as the first novel to use purely American themes, *The Spy* presents Betty (not Betsy) Flanagan as a military widow running a hotel in Four Corners. Although bibulous and slatternly, she has a stout patriot's heart. In addition, "Betty had the merit of being the inventor of that beverage which is so well-known at the present hour, to all the patriots who make a winter's march between the commercial and political capitals of this great state, and which is distinguished by the name of 'cocktail.'" Cooper remains tantalizingly silent on the sort of drinks his character serves, but he does mention that from her Virginia customers, Betty picked up the habit of using mint.

All this is interesting, but is it history? We know that Cooper relied on the oral testimony of Revolutionary War veterans in assembling material for *The Spy*, and that most of its locations and characters are rooted in historical fact. It is therefore possible that an old soldier credited Flanagan with inventing the cocktail, but even that much is pure speculation.

Frustration in the search for the word's origin has driven even respected lexicographers to some wild leaps. Richard Manning Chapman, who helped John Russell Bartlett compile his *Dictionary of Americanisms* (1848), speculated in his notebooks that "this term seems to have been suggested by the shape which froth, as of a glass of porter, etc., assumes when it flows over the side of the tumbler, etc., containing the liquid effervescing." The foam, he argued, looked like the docked tail of a dray horse, known as a cocktail.

In a purely fanciful vein, the *New York World* in 1891 claimed that the word was Aztec, and that the drink was invented by "a Toltec noble" who ordered his daughter, Xochitl, to bring a sample to the king. "Xochitl" became "cocktail." More recently, a linguist has suggested that the word comes from the West African *kaketal*, or scorpion, which has the sting of a well-prepared martini.

We arrive on more plausible ground with the hypothesis that "cocktail" derives from the French *coquetel*, a term for "mixed drink" current in Bordeaux and introduced to America by French soldiers fighting in the Revolutionary War. The French story has the merit of taking as its protagonist a bona fide historical figure, Antoine Peychaud, a New Orleans apothecary known for the brandy and bitters he served in eggcups known as "coquetiers." (Peychaud's bitters, an essential ingredient in the Sazerac cocktail, are still made today in New Orleans.) When pronounced by English speakers, "coquetier" became "cocktay," and from there it was but a short jump to "cocktail."

But the word may just as likely have been English in origin. "Cock ale" was ale in which a pulverized and spiced red cock has been steeped for a week or so. The recipe deserves to be recorded:

Take ten gallons of ale and a large cock, the older the better; parboil the cock, flay him, and stamp him in a stone mortar till his bones are broken (you must craw and gut him when you flay him), then put the cock into two quarts of sack, and put to it three pounds of raisins of the sun stoned, some blades of mace and a few cloves; put all these into a canvas bag, and a little before you find the ale has done working, put the ale and bag together in a vessel; in a week or nine days bottle it up, fill the bottles but just above the neck, and give it the same time to ripen as other ale.

Fascinating, but cock ale and cocktail show no meaningful similarities, unlike Peychaud's eggcup concoctions.

A more persuasive, or at least ingenious, case for the English origin of the word appears in H. L. Mencken's *The Amer-*

ican Language, which cites an unnamed Pennsylvania corre-
spondent as follows: "In many English taverns the last of the
liquors drawn from barrels of ardent spirits, otherwise the
cock-tailings, were thrown together in a common receptacle.
The mixture was sold to topers at a reduced price, so naturally
they called for *cocktails*." Mencken explained that "cock" referred to a valve or spigot, and "tailings" to dregs or leavings.

Enough. Whatever its origins, "cocktail" quickly passed
into general usage. Washington Irving, in his *History of New
York* (1809), refers to "cock-tail, stone-fence, and sherry-
cobbler" as "recondite" beverages, but within a few years the
cocktail was recondite no more. The mixed drink became universal throughout the land.

It must have tasted good ("Makes a feller wish he had a
throat a mile long and a palate at every inch of it," one early
enthusiast reported), because between the 1790s and 1830
Americans were consuming spirituous liquors at triple today's
rate. "The pocket flask has grown into a case-bottle," wrote the
temperance advocate Samuel Dexter in 1823, "and the keg into
a barrel."

No one can quite explain why, although commonsense the-
ories abound. Price was certainly no deterrent. Whiskey, un-
taxed between 1802 and 1862 except for a brief period after
the War of 1812, sold for as little as 25 cents a gallon. Drink
may have provided relief from a monotonous diet heavy on
salted meats. Constant indigestion, the natural consequence of
a leaden, fatty cuisine, created a land-office business for any
mixture that could penetrate grease and get the gastric juices
flowing. Drink offered an escape from hard, unremitting labor.
And, just as in colonial days, liquor was thought to build
strength and promote health. At least one nineteenth-century
insurance company imposed a surcharge on abstainers, who

were regarded as weak and weedy, and unquestionably a bad actuarial risk.

The morning eye-opener seemed no more remarkable to Americans of the time than a mouthwash rinse does today. The "anti-fogmatic," taken as directed ("in exact proportion to the thickness of the fog," according to the *Massachusetts Spy* in 1789), was thought to ward off the fever and ague that a fog in the throat could cause. In 1821, the *Lancaster Journal* in Pennsylvania provided a humorous taxonomy of the anti-fogmatic, dividing it into four genuses: gum-tickler ("warms the gums, and removes bad taste from the mouth after sleeping"), phlegm cutter, gall breaker, and clear comforter. Twenty species were enumerated as well.

Visitors to the United States almost uniformly depicted *Homo americanus* with a plug of tobacco in his cheek and whiskey on his breath, whatever the hour. By 1822, an anonymous writer was defining a simple Kentucky breakfast as "three cocktails and a chaw of terbacker." This may not have been fanciful. A tavern bill from 1812 shows that one guest consumed three mint slings before breakfast, nine tumblers of grog before dinner, three glasses of wine and bitters with dinner, and, just to put a gloss on the meal, two "ticklers" of French brandy afterward.

Perhaps what Frederick Marryat called "the pleasantness, amenity, and variety of the potations" had something to do with the rise in consumption, although here the historian sees through a shot glass, darkly. The bittered sling seems to have been universal, as was its close cousin, the mint julep. Punches and cobblers—wine or spirits, sugar, and a festive garnish of fruits—are frequently cited. Likewise the Stone Fence, also known as the Stone Wall, a mixture of brandy and cider. But recipes are rarely to be found. Dickens, in his 1842 tour of the

United States, encountered something called the Timber Doodle in Boston. Alas, he failed to record the ingredients.

The lack of evidence is frustrating, because it is precisely in this period that ice enters the picture, a giant step in the cocktail's evolution. Ice was not unknown, of course, even to the colonists. Well-to-do farmers in the Northeast maintained pondside icehouses, and hotels depended on ice deliveries for food preservation. But ice remained a luxury for most citizens. When available, it went to produce ice cream. "Ice was jewelry," Mark Twain wrote. "Only the rich could wear it."

But after the 1830s, with the invention of the ice plow, ice harvesting became a commercial proposition. Production soared, and the price dropped—enough to influence the preparation of mixed drinks. In 1835, a citation appears for the Hailstorm (or Hailstone)—spirits chilled with small lumps of ice. The Snowstorm (ingredients unknown) appears to be a chilly relative from the same period.

Exactly when and where ice first hit glass is impossible to say, for the chilling of the cocktail had already taken place by 1862, when Jerry Thomas published *How to Mix Drinks, or The Bon-Vivant's Companion*, America's first book of cocktail recipes. His book and its imitators called for ice in all forms. Cocktails were made with shaved, broken, and cracked ice, with lumps both large and small. The bartender and his assistants worked with ice pick, shaver, and mallet on a large cake, sometimes encased in a canvas money sack. In proper establishments, the final product was washed before being deposited in the patron's glass with an ice scoop or pair of tongs. Gradually, ice came to be regarded not as a flashy option but as an essential ingredient. Cocktails, the dictionary writers agreed, had to be cold. John S. Farmer, the English lexicographer, defined a cocktail in his 1889 dictionary as a wineglassful of brandy, whiskey, gin, or other spirit mixed with a teaspoonful of bitters (usually Angostura), a pinch of sugar, and crushed ice. In the same year, the *Century Dictionary* defined "cocktail" as "an American drink, strong, stimulating, and cold."

The introduction of ice had the transforming effect of electricity on city streets. The bittered sling took on an entirely different character when mixed with crushed ice. It became fresher, more exciting, racy. A new sense of energy emanated from the cocktail, as the limitless possibilities of the form opened up. With the rise of the city and an industrial economy, the pace of invention accelerated, and the cocktail entered its era of greatness.

FOUR

SWINGING DOORS

I doted on the cool, refreshing scent of a good saloon on a hot summer day.
—H. L. Mencken, *Happy Days* (1940)

The saloon must go.
—Motto of the Anti-Saloon League

The cocktail, a gifted but struggling amateur in the early days of the republic, came into its own with the rise of the saloon in the nineteenth century. Like most of our national institutions, the saloon evolved gradually, nourished by English roots yet reaching instinctively toward a purely American form. Over time, the colonial tavern, which offered food, drink, and shelter, found some of its functions taken over by more specialized operations: the hotel, the restaurant, and the saloon, a temple of drink presided over by a kind of democratic high priest, the bartender.

The word "saloon" conjures up a picture of swinging doors, player pianos, and six-shooters, but its spirit and its origins are urban. Long before rude entrepreneurs on the mining frontier were pitching canvas tents and dispensing whiskey from the barrel, the saloon was a glittering palace on city streets, a sparkling wonderland of cut crystal, polished brass, and silver mirrors. By the time Prohibition arrived, the saloon would be synonymous with drinking at its worst: a reeking dive dispensing rotgut at a few cents a shot. In the popular mind, it seduced the workingman into throwing away his meager wage and put the nation's youth on the fast track to hell. But the saloon did not start out that way.

On a summer day in 1839, an Austrian traveler named Francis Grund decided to escape the sweltering heat of Manhattan by heading to the north shore of Staten Island, where pleasure boats stopped at a hotel known as the Pavilion. There he found the American saloon at its finest. Wines and spirits from all over the world were arrayed behind the bar, set off by lemons and oranges carefully stacked in pyramids. Because of the heat, the Pavilion was doing a land-office business in mint juleps. The newcomer spied "a huge mass of ice and a forest of mint, together with two large bottles of French and peach brandy."

Not many Americans had seen anything quite so impressive, but as the century wore on, fancy saloons appeared in every American city. They were intended to dazzle, in the Victorian manner, with an all-out decorative onslaught. Woodwork was massive, ceilings high, glassware ornate. "I have visited in my day the barrooms of all civilized countries," Mencken wrote in the 1940s, "but none that I ever saw came within miles of a high-toned American saloon of the Golden Age. Today the influence of the cocktail lounge has brought in blue glass, chrome fixtures, and bars of puny and pale woods, but in the time I speak of, saloon architects stuck to mirrors as

God first made them, to honest brass, and to noble and imper-
ishable mahogany."

Even the lesser fry made some gesture, however feeble,
toward monumental effect. In the same way that every American town billed itself as the fastest-growing burg in the nation,
all saloons claimed to have a bar of epic proportions. In the
West, land of the tall tale and the big brag, rare was the establishment that did not advertise its mile-long bar, which, although longer than the mile-long hot dog, usually measured a
hundred feet or so. In Portland, Oregon, however, thirsty log-
gers could belly up to 684 feet of solid mahogany at Erickson's
on Burnside Street.

The fanciest bars were found in the grand hotels, which op-
erated as semipublic institutions. Anyone, guest or not, felt free
to stroll into a fine hotel lobby, settle down in a comfortable
chair, and read a newspaper—or even write a letter or two on
the house stationery. The bars and restaurants of the top hotels

---

After due reflection he first sought out "Emerald Pat" Kerrigan, whom he
knew personally but with whom he was by no means intimate politically,
at his "Emporium Bar" in Dearborn Street. This particular saloon, a feature of political Chicago at this time, was a large affair containing
among other marvelous saloon fixtures a circular bar of cherry wood
twelve feet in diameter, which glowed as a small mountain with the cus-
tomary plain and colored glasses, bottles, labels, and mirrors. The floor
was a composition of small, shaded red-and-green marbles; the ceiling a
daub of pinky, fleshy nudes floating among diaphanous clouds; the walls
were alternate panels of cerise and brown set in rosewood. Mr. Kerrigan, when other duties were not pressing, was usually to be found standing chatting with several friends and surveying the wonders of his bar
trade, which was very large.

—Theodore Dreiser, *The Titan* (1914)

served as rallying points for captains of industry, moneymen, journalists, and political fat cats. The Amen Corner, two pairs of red plush settees just outside the bar of the Fifth Avenue Hotel in Manhattan, saw nearly as much high-level political dealing as the halls of Congress. The Republican State Committee maintained its headquarters there for years, and when the hotel closed in 1908, the settees were formally donated to the Museum of the City of New York and the New-York Historical Society.

The most celebrated of the swank bars could be found at New York's Hoffman House, which opened in the fall of 1864. Located on Broadway at Twenty-fifth Street, the hotel had a long mahogany bar at which seventeen bartenders worked, their images reflected in wall mirrors said to be the largest in America. The mirrors ran a poor second, however, to Bouguereau's beguiling *Nymphs and Satyr*. Florid, overblown, and frankly erotic, the painting simply overpowered the bar's other paintings, even the nude-intensive *Vision of Faust*.

It was the age of "more is more," and not only in decoration. America took an uncomplicated attitude toward wealth and display. When the rich ate, they did not pick at a minimalist arrangement of microgreens and baby vegetables. They gorged. They sat down to epic, heart-stopping meals that could make oak tables sag. The fat sizzled, the wine flowed in torrents, and entire animal populations suffered drastic decline. There was nothing furtive about any of this. The oxymoronic notion of intimate public space did not exist. Life outside the home was lived on a theatrical, even heroic scale. It was an age of high living and free spending, of large men with large appetites. "Them was the days when everybody drank champagne," one Hoffman House bartender recalled wistfully, looking back from the dismal Depression year of 1930.

For pure, gorgeous, unfettered display, for the sheer exuberance of wealth, the United States has never really matched its performance in the period between the Civil War and World War I. In 1860, there were perhaps twenty millionaires in America; by 1880 there were a hundred, a number that would increase to more than four thousand in 1890 and forty thousand in 1916. Cheap labor and no income tax allowed the rich to live like kings, and their opulent style set the tone. Not many New York swells could afford to spend $100,000 on a dinner at Delmonico's, like Diamond Jim Brady, but they could and did stand rounds for the house and call out for quarts of champagne. The great saloons provided a gaudy stage for the grand gesture.

The Hoffman House, a favorite with Democratic politicians, the Tammany machine, and the sporting element, prided itself on its fine wines and liquors. William F. Mulhall, who began tending bar at the hotel in 1882, recalled Rhine wine at eighteen dollars a bottle, the equivalent of two hundred dollars today. Brandy came in a little stone jug at fifty cents, although the bar kept a fifty-year-old Hennessy cognac, which it served at a dollar a drink—"the highest price ever known for a drink of liquor in America up to that time," Mulhall wrote. The unsuspecting customer who pounded his fist on the bar and demanded the best drink in the house sometimes wound up with a bill at the end of the evening that sobered him up fast.

The splurge drink was champagne, and it flowed through the cities of late-nineteenth-century America like a mighty, foaming river. Money and champagne always find each other. In the roaring eighties of the twentieth century, Dom Perignon—D.P. for short—became the Gatorade of the Wall Street warrior, the official beverage of the stock market Olympics. Roederer Cristal, likewise, became emblematic of the coke-fueled Hollywood party. A century earlier, the booming market and an expanding industrial economy demanded champagne, and lots of it. Consumption was boosted by gregarious wine buyers, familiar figures in all the better saloons. A cross between a door-to-door salesman and a professional host, the wine buyer would treat lavishly with the champagne he represented, then move along to the next bar up the street. Ordering a quart bottle rather than a pint marked a customer as a "sport." A half-gallon magnum, one memoirist wrote, "was the special 'tour de force' of the high roller, the wine agent, and the spender."

For every Hoffman House, of course, there were a thousand humble corner saloons, with a long, scuffed wooden bar and sawdust on the floor. Over the bar hung two works of art, a voluptuous Venus and John L. Sullivan, in fighting posture. Behind the bar were humorous cards on the order of IF DRINKING INTERFERES WITH YOUR BUSINESS, CUT OUT BUSINESS.

"When you had visited one of the old-time saloons, you had seen a thousand," wrote George Ade, the Indiana satirist, in his dry-eyed history of the pre-Prohibition bar.

> Very often it stood on a corner so as to have two street entrances and wave a gilded beer sign at pedestrians drifting along from any point of the compass. The entrance was through swinging doors which were shuttered so that anyone standing on the outside could not see what was happening on the inside. The windows were masked by grille work, potted ferns, one-sheet posters, and a fly-specked array of fancy-shaped bottles which were merely symbols and not merchandise.

Cocktails were for sissies. The drinks were whiskey, drunk straight, and beer. Branded whiskeys were for the select few.

Most customers ordered rye or bourbon, distinguishable by the shapes of their bottles, which were filled from two-gallon or three-gallon jugs, which in turn were filled from barrels in the basement. The bartender placed a two-and-a-half-ounce glass on the bar, with water on the side. The customer poured his own. Anyone asking for a mixed drink would have to live with the results. "The plain sturdy bartender of our neighborhood," wrote a Cincinnatian looking back at the 1880s saloon, "was likely to come up with a mixture made by guess and by God."

Out west, the set-up could be even more primitive: a canvas tent and a few barrels dispensing "cowboy cocktails," or straight whiskey. But the iconic saloon of the B Western should not be taken at face value. True, the earliest bars were as crude as their customers and their whiskey, which was prized for strength, not subtlety. The right stuff—perhaps alcohol enlivened with red pepper and tobacco—was known as "40 rod" (powerful enough to stun a man at that distance), "extract of scorpions," "chain lightning," "stagger juice," or "panther's breath." A shot, it was said, could "draw a blood blister on a rawhide boot." Sometimes the whiskey tasted like the boot. In the Klondike, gold miners added piquancy to their whiskey by throwing unwashed foot rags into the mash.

But there's ample evidence that the Western saloon could be fancy enough for the most persnickety Eastern dude. San Francisco rivaled New York and New Orleans for luxury in matters of food and drink, but even lesser towns could offer the visitor a top-flight saloon with a professional bartender in full command of the drink repertoire. Hinton Helper, a Southerner who toured California in the early 1850s, decided that his readers might like to know the bill of fare at a San Francisco saloon called the Blue Wing. His list ran to more than a hundred drinks, including such colorful but long-forgotten thirst-quenchers as the Flip Flap, One-eyed Joe, Ne Plus Ultra, and Red Light. Helper also noted, with some alarm, that somewhere between twelve and fifteen thousand Californians were engaged in the liquor trade, in a state whose total population was only 250,000. San Francisco alone was reported to have 743 bartenders in 1853.

San Francisco, the queen of cities, was unique. But even out in the bush, a thirsty stranger could expect something better than warm beer when he walked into a bar. Corvelo, California, could not have been a sophisticated metropolis in 1873, but a writer for *Harper's* was handed the following gilt-edged "Toddy Time-Table" on entering the local saloon:

6 a.m. Eye Opener

7 a.m. Appetizer

8 a.m. Digester

9 a.m. Big Reposer

10 a.m. Refresher

11 a.m. Stimulant

12 m. Ante-Lunch

1 p.m. Settler

2 p.m. à la Smythe

3 p.m. Cobbler

4 p.m. Social Drink

5 p.m. Invigorator

6 p.m. Solid Straight

7 p.m. Chit-chat

8 p.m. Fancy Smile

9 p.m. Entire [*sic*] Act

10 p.m. Sparkler

11 p.m. Rouser

12 a.m. Night Cap

It is possible, of course, that the dedicated patrons of this saloon stuck to a shot of "tornado juice" throughout the busy
day, but the schedule suggests a taste for finer things.

The most famous feature of the saloon was the free lunch.
As nearly as anyone can tell, the practice began in New Orleans in the late 1830s at the Café des Réfugiés, where the
management began offering a midday menu of soup, a piece
of beef or ham with potatoes, meat pie, and oyster patties.
Not surprisingly, business picked up. Soon the practice spread
throughout the city and beyond.

For decades afterward, a glass of beer was a ticket to a side
table loaded down with the fixings for a noontime feast. At the
more expensive establishments, the food was good—so good
that one turn-of-the-century observer could not figure out
where the profit lay. "You pay ten cents for a glass of beer and
you tip the waiter ten cents," he wrote. "For his ten cents the
waiter brings you a napkin, a fifty-cent slice of roast beef,
twenty-five cents worth of potatoes, ten cents worth of beets,
five cents worth of bread, and ten cents worth of cheese." The
lunch table at the old Waldorf in New York, offering canapés,
anchovies, Virginia ham, and assorted cheeses and crudités,
cost the hotel $75,000 a year.

But the more typical nickel-a-beer saloons offered a humble spread of soup or chowder, ham, hot dogs, baked beans,
pretzels, dried herring, pickles, or head cheese, all heavily
salted to encourage another round of drinks. At some bars, patrons could expect nothing more than cheese, stale crackers,
and onions. At the low end of the market, proprietors regarded
the free lunch as a necessary evil, and did not spend a lot of
time on the niceties. Nearly all commentators on the old saloon
recall with a shudder of disgust the communal serving fork
kept in a goblet of swampy water. Even so, bartenders had to

keep a sharp eye out for the "free lunch fiend" who would si-
dle up to the lunch counter without a drink.

Nostalgia for the saloon gripped many American men during the arid years of Prohibition, a testing time that lasted
from 1920 to 1934. Selective recall smoothed over the rough
spots and caused the more attractive features to shine with a
double luster. The aroma of stale beer and sawdust lived in the
memory as a heavenly scent, ripe with promise of boon com-
panionship and lively but undemanding conversation. In bygone days, when the workingman lived in a cramped, dismal
tenement, and the middle-class home lacked the technological
delights that dazzle the present age, the corner bar beckoned
seductively. All but the most abject bars offered at least the
pretense of splendor and elegance. For an hour or two, the man
of small means could live like a nabob, surrounded by shim-
mering glass and polished wood, waited on by a professional in
starched linen.

But there was more to it than that. The saloon was a democratic arena in which a man could count on being taken at his
own valuation, a place where his opinion counted for just as
much as that of the fellow next to him. Freed from the de-
meaning hierarchies of the workplace, men could mingle and
philosophize as equals. At home and at work, the average man
cut a less than heroic figure. The saloon offered escape, the opportunity to project a different, more dashing image before an
uncritical audience. It might be said that only in the saloon
could a man reach his full potential. There, in the midst of ap-
proving peers—the kind of fellows who could be counted on to
laugh even when they'd heard the joke before—he could
glance in the mirror and see reflected a masculine paragon: a
wit, a bit of a rogue, and still, all things considered, surprisingly youthful. All this for the price of a beer.

FIVE

THE ICEMAN COMETH

Bartending is an old and honorable trade.
—Patrick Gavin Duffy,
The Official Mixer's Manual (1934)

When Francis Grund took in the scene at the Pavilion in 1839, he found himself fascinated by the frantic activity of the man behind the bar, "preparing ice-punch, mint-juleps, port and madeira *sangarie*, apple toddy, gin sling, etc., with a celerity of motion of which I had heretofore scarcely seen an example." Here was something strange and wonderful: a man whose sole occupation was to mix outlandish drinks. He was the bartender, equal parts chef, juggler, and magician, the unsung hero of the cocktail's golden age.

Whence he came, no one knows. The word "bartender" first appears in 1836, but the origins of the profession remain obscure, and the early practitioners of the trade can be seen only by a fitful, flickering light—in the chance remarks of a traveler like Grund or the brief descriptive passage of a novelist.

He was a commanding, even aristocratic figure, dressed in a sparkling white tunic, generally sporting a handlebar mustache with waxed ends, his cuffs kept free of the glassware by ornamental sleeve garters. He was sommelier, actor, and shaman, an adept in the arcana of the cocktail, a repository of sporting knowledge, and a master of the art of conversing without ever expressing an opinion.

Early observers marveled at the barman's flashy technique. In Hawthorne's *Blithedale Romance* (1852), the narrator chances to observe a master at work: "With a tumbler in each hand he tossed the contents from one to the other. Never conveying it awry, nor spilling the least drop, he compelled the frothy liquor, as it seemed to me, to spout forth from one glass and descend into the other, in a great parabolic curve, as well-defined and calculable as a planet's orbit."

The use of tumblers rather than a shaker was standard mixing practice. The silver cocktail shaker, now as much a part of the cocktail's iconography as the martini glass, did not come along until the 1870s.

The *Police Gazette* showcased the middling sort of mixologist who flourished around the turn of the century. The weekly paper, devoted to lurid crimes, boxing (or "the fistic arts"), and the female form, regularly featured local bartenders from around the country, along with drink recipes sent in by mail, as many as a dozen in each issue. A few paragraphs of praise for the bartender's skill would lead up to the ultimate character reference: "He is a good fellow."

The modern bartender is regarded as a kind of valet, but a century ago, he was a man of substance. "In Nevada, for a time, the lawyer, the editor, the banker, the chief desperado, the chief gambler, and the saloon-keeper occupied the same level in society, and it was the highest," Mark Twain wrote in *Roughing It*:

The cheapest and easiest way to become an influential man and be looked up to by the community at large was to stand behind a bar, wear a cluster diamond pin, and sell whiskey. I am not sure but that the saloon-keeper held a shade higher rank than any other member of society. His opinion had weight. It was his privilege to say how the elections should go. No great movement could succeed without the countenance and direction of the saloon-keepers. It was a high favor when the chief saloon-keeper consented to serve in the legislature or the board of aldermen.

Some bartenders achieved celebrity status. The most famous of them all was Jerry Thomas, whose career sheds light on the profession at its higher reaches. Born in 1830 in Watertown, New York, Thomas went to sea as a young man and washed ashore in San Francisco in 1849, where he became first assistant to the principal bartender at the El Dorado Hotel. After panning for gold, he opened up a mining-town saloon and, by his own account, presented the first minstrel show in California. Returning east with a bankroll of $16,000, he opened a bar under P. T. Barnum's museum on lower Broadway.

Thomas was a restless sort. In 1853 he headed south to Charleston, where he tended bar at the Mills House; then he moved west to Chicago. After mixing drinks in Chicago, he moved on to St. Louis, where he served as head bartender at the Planters Hotel. Tiring of St. Louis, he went down to New Orleans and opened a saloon, then headed back to San Francisco but soon returned to New York, where he became principal bartender at the Metropolitan Hotel and patented his own brand of bitters. So great was Thomas's renown that in 1859 he toured Europe carrying a $4,000 set of custom-made silver bar implements, with which he demonstrated the American art of the cocktail to curious Londoners and Parisians.

Thomas's chief rival was Harry Johnson, author of *The New and Improved Illustrated Bartender's Manual*. Little is known of Johnson, although a fine photographic portrait graces his book, showing a powerfully built man with a thick handlebar mustache. By his own account he traveled widely, and he may have crossed paths with Thomas in San Francisco in the 1860s.

It is a fact that from 1882 to 1887 Johnson ran the Little Jumbo on the Bowery, a saloon that enticed passersby with a sidewalk advertisement showing the dozens of cocktails on offer. Although evidence is scant, it's not hard to guess that Johnson was a vain, prickly man. The introduction to his bartender's manual takes an oddly bellicose tone, daring readers to find fault with a single one of his recipes, and leafing through the advertisements at the back of the 1888 edition, one finds a truculent announcement by Johnson himself, emphasizing that "since May 1, 1887, I have had positively no connection with the Little Jumbo at 119 Bowery." The wording suggests a rancorous split.

The sense that he was playing Salieri to Thomas's Mozart must have rankled. The copy of his bar guide in Harvard's Widener Library includes a strange, pasted-in addendum from the publisher in which Johnson claims that his book was originally published in San Francisco in 1860—two years earlier than Thomas's guide—making it the first book of its kind. No one has ever seen such an edition. He also boasted that in 1869 he was challenged by five of the finest bartenders in the United States to take part in a tournament of skill in New Orleans, "with the consequence that to me was awarded the championship of the United States."

In 1882, the *New York Sun* caught up with Jerry Thomas at

his bar on Broadway at Twenty-second Street, not far from the Hoffman House. Thomas, in the midst of shifting location to Sixth Avenue across from the Jefferson Market police station, was preparing to auction off some of the pictures by Thomas Nast and others that had made his bar a kind of tourist attraction as well as a watering hole.

The bartender, now fifty-two, cut a curious figure, holding forth "as two white rats pretty enough to be guinea pigs cut capers upon his shoulders, caressed him at the corners of his mustache, and mounted occasionally to the top of his derby hat." On a nearby wall hung the centerpiece of his art collection, a painting titled *Jerry Thomas's Original Dream*, showing the celebrated barman in an armchair, surrounded by famous Americans.

Who's to say Thomas didn't earn his seat among the great? To be recognized as America's greatest bartender counted for something. Standards of the profession were high. At the finer saloons, where an apprenticeship of two years was not uncommon, bartenders spent hours refining the visual presentation of the bar, ensuring a pleasing spectacle of sparkling glassware, attractive fruit, and clean, starched linen. (A cocktail often came with a cloth napkin for dabbing at one's mustache.) The cash register was a rarity until the 1880s, which perhaps accounts for the allure of the bartending profession, since the honor system allowed for robust self-tipping.

The old-time bartender probably deserved the spare change. He had to know his drinks, in an age when tastes inclined toward the baroque. Consider the Gladstone, an 1890s cocktail. The drink required two dashes of sugar syrup (called "gum" in the old recipe books), a dash of maraschino liqueur, two dashes of bitters, one dash of absinthe, and equal parts whiskey, Jamaica rum, and Russian kümmel. There were many drinks of this kind. According to Albert Stevens Crockett, in his history of the old Waldorf bar, "Certain of those bartenders knew how to make, and did make, 271 different kinds of cocktails. They knew how to compose, and did compose, 491 different kinds of mixed drinks."

The mixing of a cocktail was a matter for professionals. A man would no sooner shake one up himself than cut his own hair or bake his own soufflé. Jack London had his cocktails mixed by an Oakland bartender and shipped to him in bulk. Fear of mixing created a business opportunity that the Heublein Company of Hartford seized upon with great success. In 1892 it began marketing Club Cocktails, a line of seven bottled drinks: the York, Manhattan, martini, whiskey, Holland gin, Old Tom gin, and vermouth cocktails. (The York, now forgotten, was three parts French vermouth to one part maraschino, with several dashes of orange bitters; the Holland and Old Tom were simply dry and sweet gin cocktails; and the whiskey cocktail would nowadays be called an old-fashioned, which is shorthand for old-fashioned whiskey cocktail.)

The 1862 edition of Thomas's *How to Mix Drinks* listed 236 beverages but only ten cocktails: the bottle, brandy, fancy brandy, whiskey, champagne, gin, fancy gin, Japanese, soda, and Jersey. (A Japanese cocktail was brandy with orgeat syrup, bitters, sugar, and a lemon twist, while the Jersey called for cider, bitters, sugar, and a lemon twist.) As a category, the cocktail shared space with punches, flips, toddies, crustas, slings, and sangarees. When Thomas came out with new editions in 1876 and 1887, the number of cocktails had doubled, and the total number of drinks had swelled to more than three hundred.

The lexicographers reflect this creative explosion. The 1848 edition of Bartlett's *Dictionary of Americanisms* includes only a few drink-related words, like "cocktail," "cobbler," and "sling," but the 1877 edition lists Thomas's ten cocktails and throws in another 130, among them the Ching Ching, the Deadbeat, the Fiscal Agent, the Moral Suasion, the Ropee, the Shambro, the Split Ticket, and the Vox Populi. Just twelve years later, a rival lexicographer called Bartlett's list ridiculously incomplete.

In his introduction to the cocktail section of his book, Thomas stated that "the cocktail is a modern invention, and is generally used on fishing and other sporting parties," which suggests that just after mid-century, the individually prepared drink served across the bar was no means universal. And indeed, Thomas devotes an entire chapter to cocktails meant to be bottled and taken along on outings. An ingenious product for the outdoor drinker was made by the Vinous Rubber Grape Company of Philadelphia, which in 1885 patented a rubber capsule filled with spirits or wine. The buyer popped one in his mouth, bit down for a quick, stimulating burst, and then spit out the emptied capsule.

It is impossible to know how representative Thomas's recipes are. The 1876 and 1887 editions include, in recognizable form, a few classics, like the Manhattan and the Tom Collins. But they are the exceptions. Most of the drinks reflect a national sweet tooth. Gum, a sugar syrup thickened with gum arabic, is used liberally, and when gin is called for, it is usually the sweet variety known as Old Tom. The cocktails that are not sweet tend to be complex, calling for ingredients like arrack, orgeat, snakeroot, or tansy.

Thomas's most famous contribution to the cocktail repertoire was the Blue Blazer, equal parts Scotch and boiling water set alight and poured back and forth from one tumbler to another in a continuous stream of fire. The trick can be done with practice. Although the diluted whiskey barely catches fire, the back-and-forth pouring acts as a kind of bellows, creating a roaring fire. A period engraving shows Thomas, arms outstretched, generating a fiery cataract some five feet long, as three swells look on admiringly.

The pyrotechnics of the American bartender and his bizarre concoctions seem to have passed unnoticed on native soil. Abroad, Uncle Sam's mixmasters created a sensation, setting up shop and stunning Europeans with drinks like the Connecticut Eye-Opener, the Alabama Fog-Cutter, and the Lightning Smash. The names suggest that the Americans were determined to give Europe its money's worth, to assure it that the United States was indeed a wonderland of vulgar surprises.

All sorts of strange cocktails made the rounds, and most of them were on display at the Exposition Universelle in Paris in 1867, where the U.S. offerings included a genuine American restaurant and bar dispensing New World drinks, both alcoholic and nonalcoholic. On one busy day the bartenders went through five hundred bottles of sherry for sherry cobblers, a drink that was served with a straw, to the amusement of the French. A cartoon in the satirical magazine *Charivari* showed a small boy staring at a cobbler drinker, convinced that he is watching a glass-blowing exhibition.

George Augustus Sala, a well-known British journalist, reported on the exposition's more memorable sights. The American bar definitely qualified:

> At the bar, and from siphon tubes decorated with silvery figures of the American eagle, were dispensed the delicious "cream soda" so highly recommended by the faculty. "Cobblers," "noggs," "smashes," "cocktails," "eye-openers," "moustache twisters," and "corpse revivers" were also on hand; and I dare say you might have obtained the mystic "tip and tic," the exhilarating "morning glory," the mild but health-giving sarsaparilla

punch, to say nothing of "one of them things," which is a recondite and almost inscrutable drink.

The Tip and Tic has disappeared without a trace. But the Morning Glory appears in Jerry Thomas's book, where the recipe calls for one pony each of brandy and whiskey, three dashes of gum syrup, two dashes of curaçao, two dashes of bitters, one dash of absinthe, and a lemon twist.

Sala may have been amused, but some of his countrymen took a dim view of America's contributions in the drink line. Thomas Hughes, the author of *Tom Brown's Schooldays*, dropped by the American bar at the Paris exposition and tried a coffee cocktail (a port-based drink named for its color, not its ingredients). He hated it. The coffee cocktail, he wrote, was the worst thing he'd tasted since castor oil. In *Cups and Their Customs*, two English writers, Henry Porter and George Roberts, deplored what they called "the sensation drinks" sent over by the Americans. "We will pass the American bar, with its bad brandies and fiery wine," they wrote, "and express our gratitude at the slight success which 'Pick-me-up,' 'Corpse-reviver,' 'Chain-lightning,' and the like, have had in this country."

Improbably, the Corpse Reviver really did exist. It was equal parts noyau (a sweet almond liqueur), maraschino, and yellow Chartreuse, poured carefully to form three distinct color bands. The drink must have found favor with the French, for some thirty years after the Paris exposition, an American strolling along the rue Auger noticed an American bar that offered a long list of arresting drinks. Sure enough, along with the Bosom Caresser, Flip Flap, Heap of Comfort, and Flash of Lightning, the menu included the well-traveled Corpse Reviver.

The American cocktail gained ground rapidly. Foreigners

found them fascinating, and American travelers abroad demanded them. An American businessman touring Australia and the Far East in 1857 noted in his diary that although Australians seemed indifferent to American liquors, they were enthusiastic about American mixed drinks. In England, the mixed drink made an impression early on, perhaps because of Thomas's international tour, although Thomas does not appear to have been the first to shake up a drink on British soil. A satirical sketch in Dickens's weekly journal *Household Words* in 1851 presents an old-time London pub owner lamenting the fad for American drinks like gin slings, brandy cocktails, and mint juleps. The preface to the 1862 edition of Thomas's book mentions a bar near the Bank of England where an American bartender attracted a crowd with newfangled cocktails, and by 1863, the renowned chef Charles Francatelli, in *The Cook's Guide and Housekeeper's and Butler's Assistant,* devoted a chapter to American drinks, including well-known mixtures like the gin sling and mint julep, along with less obvious ones like the Sleeper, the Floster, and the Knickerbocker. The recipes are bizarre. His julep, for example, calls for orange rind, orange juice, gin, and sherry. In fact, the only thing it has in common with a mint julep is mint. The main point is that Francatelli, as early as 1863, felt that he needed to address the issue of American drinks. God forbid that an unsuspecting butler should falter when an American guest demanded a Locomotive cocktail. The image of the American bartender, twin shakers in hand, was so well established, in fact, that in 1862 *Punch* ran a scathing caricature of Abraham Lincoln behind the bar, shaking up a cocktail from bottles labeled "brag," "bunkum," and "bosh."

In 1874, the Criterion restaurant in Piccadilly imported an American, Leo Engel, and opened an American bar on its ground floor. For the first time, London had a top-quality showcase for American cocktails. Engel went on to publish a recipe book, *American and Other Drinks*, in 1880. It borrowed liberally, even shamelessly, from Jerry Thomas. Recipe theft was rife among publishers of drink books, and Engel's made little effort to conceal his crimes. Mississippi Punch became Missouri Punch, Bottled Velvet was renamed Bottled Silk, and dozens of other recipes were simply lifted intact.

The American bar proved so popular that in 1898 the Savoy Hotel opened its own, and the Berkeley followed suit within a few years. From 1903 to 1924, the Savoy's head bartender was a woman, Ada Coleman. She passed the silver shaker to Harry Craddock, a former bartender at the Holland House in New York, who crossed the Atlantic when Prohibition robbed him of his trade. Following in Engel's footsteps, Craddock committed his recipes to print in *The Savoy Cocktail Book* (1930), perhaps the most stylish drink book ever produced. Craddock brought to England the American trick of creating cocktails for special occasions, or naming them after celebrities, a practice that caught on and held on long after bartenders in America had lost the art.

Craddock was one of the last of a breed. The enthusiasm for American drinks and American bartenders in Europe must have been bittersweet, a reminder that the American cocktail, in all its glory, was a royal exile, forcibly exported by tragic events at home. In a matter of decades, the cocktail had come full circle. From an American novelty, it had become a fixture throughout Europe. And back in America, it was in desperate straits.

SIX

THE GOLDEN AGE

When the office clock is showing
That the time is half past four,
I feel I must be going
Where I've often gone before,
For I need no rough awakening,
And I want no whistle's hoot,
To say my thirst needs slaking
On the Cocktail Route.
—From Roland Whittle,
    "The Cocktail Route,"
    San Francisco News Letter,
    December 12, 1904

The "sensation" cocktails that inspired English sneers did not really represent American taste. For the most part they were showpieces, intended to astound and entertain, like the passing fads of the present-day bar—what bartenders today dismiss as "umbrella drinks." American drinks could be ornate, and bartenders put on more of a show than they do today, but in practice, the cocktail repertoire relied on fairly streamlined classics based on bourbon, rye, or gin.

At the Hoffman House, according to William Mulhall, the cocktails most in demand in the 1880s were the old-fashioned, the absinthe cocktail, martinis both dry and sweet, the vermouth cocktail, the Bronx (orange juice, gin, and equal parts sweet and dry vermouth), and the Turf Club (equal parts Plymouth gin and French vermouth with two dashes each of orange bitters, maraschino, and absinthe). New York's Continental Hotel was renowned for its whiskey sours.

Rum, by this time, was out of bounds, a low-rent option for the down-and-out. The pride of colonial America had become a prohibitionist expletive. Indeed, during the 1900 presidential campaign, Republicans could think of no better way to promote their candidate than to chant: "McKinley drinks soda water, Bryan drinks rum; McKinley is a gentleman, Bryan is a bum."

If the mainstream cocktails tended to be fairly simple, the old-time bartender nevertheless worked with a more extensive

---

Without actually deciding to do so, Charley Simmons picked a cocktail off a passing waiter's tray. It was a concoction of Bacardi, lemon juice, and a dash of Pernod, so pleasant to the taste that although he was usually a slow as well as a moderate drinker, he tossed off two Delmonico glasses in less than fifteen minutes.

"Charley, you with a cocktail?" said Hubert Ward.

"Me with a cocktail. Don't you think I'm entitled, Hubie?"

"Sure. Who better?"

"That's the way I look at it. Have you had one? It's made of Bacardi rum and it has absinthe in it. You know, Pernod. I have a feeling they're probably stronger than they taste, but if it knocks me on my can I won't play polo this afternoon."

—John O'Hara, *The Big Laugh* (1962)

battery of flavorings and extracts than his modern-day counterpart. He had at his disposal more than a dozen different bitters, and the older bar books are sprinkled with such exotica as
calisaya, crème de violette, and groseille syrup.

Absinthe, according to Mulhall, did not become popular
until the late 1890s, but when it caught on, it created a stir.
Now but a dim, lurid memory, the light-green liqueur was
made by distilling an infusion of alcohol and the leaves, root,
or bark of wormwood (*Artemesia absinthium*), hyssop, and
mint, with angelica root, sweet flag, dittany leaves, star anise,
and fennel. The result was a potent drink of 140 to 160 proof,
with a flavor resembling Pernod. The problem lay in thujone,
a fragrant ketone present in wormwood oil, which acted as a
kind of hallucinogen.

The usual method of preparation was to pour a small
amount of absinthe in a wineglass, then place a perforated silver spoon containing a lump of sugar over the glass. Water
poured on the sugar would drip sweetly into the bitter absinthe. The effects of frequent use can be seen in any number
of Impressionist paintings. "People were afraid of it," Mulhall
noted, "and many fearful stories were told of its effects on
French drinkers. But it was too seductive to be barred." He
served it in a dozen different cocktails, the most popular being
Absinthe Frappé, Absinthe Panache, Absinthe California, and
Absinthe Drip.

Mulhall claimed that the celebrated Manhattan cocktail,
long a rival to the martini, was invented by a man named
Black who kept a saloon on Broadway just below Houston
Street. This runs counter to the more popular theory that the
drink was created at the Manhattan Club in 1874, at a banquet
to celebrate Governor Tilden's election victory. The club's official history simply asserts that the cocktail was invented on its

premises, providing no date, and then gives the recipe: equal parts whiskey and vermouth, plus orange bitters. Slow evolution has transformed the drink into two parts whiskey, one part vermouth, with Angostura bitters. (The disappearance of orange bitters, which was also standard in many old martini recipes, is a sad footnote in the history of American drink.)

If the club's account was sketchy on the Manhattan, it does cite a slew of other cocktails first created at the club's bar: the Sam Ward (yellow Chartreuse with a lemon twist); the Frappé New Orleans à la Graham (whiskey, mint, and sugar); the Royal Cup (a pint of champagne, a quart of Bordeaux, soda, one pony each of brandy and maraschino, lemon juice, sugar, mint, seasonal fruits, and a cucumber); the Manhattan cocktail à la Gilbert (whiskey, French vermouth, and Amer Picon bitters); the Manhattan Cooler à la McGregor (Scotch, soda, lemon juice, and bitters); the Columbus (whiskey, calisaya, orange bitters, acid phosphate, and a dash of curaçao); the Brut (vermouth, orange bitters, acid phosphate, and maraschino); the Riding Club (calisaya, lemon juice, and Angostura bitters); the Racquet (gin, vermouth, orange bitters, and crème de cacao); the Star (applejack, vermouth, yellow Chartreuse, and cherry bounce); the Queen Anne (brandy, vermouth, orange bitters, and maraschino); the Plimpton (Jamaica rum, vermouth, lemon juice, and orange bitters). Apparently the roll call could have gone on and on: "Indeed, the Club has drinks for every day in the year, Sundays included; for all seasons, and national, State, and city festivals."

Whatever its origins, the Manhattan seems to have reigned supreme at the Hoffman House. It came in an infinite number of varieties, and bartenders had to keep track of special formulas required by regular customers. It was the drink of the substantial man. Over at the Waldorf, J. Pierpont Morgan ordered one every day after the stock market closed.

Most of the classic cocktails, including the martini, the Manhattan, the old-fashioned, and the Bronx, were born in this high-living, fecund era. The Bronx cocktail, if Albert Stevens Crockett's *Old Waldorf Bar Days* is to be believed, was invented by Johnny Solon at the Waldorf Bar, which opened in 1897. Solon recalled that he was mixing up a Duplex—equal parts French and Italian vermouth, shaken up with a squeezed orange peel and two dashes of orange bitters—when a customer challenged him to make a new cocktail. Solon said he named the drink the Bronx because he had recently visited the Bronx Zoo. The only problem with this fascinating story is Mulhall's testimony that he was serving the drink back in the 1880s.

Whoever invented it, the drink took off. "For the Bronx was fashionable," Bernard DeVoto later wrote in *The Hour*:

The gay dogs of the Murray Hill Age drank it, the boulevardiers who wore boaters with a string to the left lapel and winked at Gibson Girls as far up Fifth Avenue as Fifty-ninth Street. It had the same cachet that Maxim's had, or Delmonico's, or say the splendid Richard Harding Davis at the more splendid Knickerbocker bar, or O. Henry in his cellar restaurant, or the bearded (or Van Dyke-ed) critics of Park Row.

Most cocktails of the period have not survived. Their very names, in many cases, suggest a limited shelf life. The cocktail instantly registered current events, celebrities, hit shows, racehorses, and the passing enthusiasms of the day. When Peary reached the North Pole, his exploit inspired the Arctic

cocktail. The Dorlando commemorated an American mara-
thon runner in the 1908 Olympics. Operettas, plays, and
musicals like *The Chocolate Soldier*, *Trilby*, *Adonis*, and *Zaza*
demanded their own drinks. The Metropole and the Normandie, New York hotels, had drinks named after them, as did
the Bijou, a Broadway theater. The Rob Roy honored the play
of the same name, while the Free Silver Fizz gave liquid expression to William Jennings Bryan's political platform.

Yale, Harvard, Princeton, and Cornell had their own cocktails, now forgotten. The Clover Club, a survivor, was the prop-
erty of the club of the same name, which met at the Bellevue
Hotel in Philadelphia. The Ward 8 sounds vaguely sinister, but
commemorates a victory celebration by the Hendricks Club, a
political operation in Boston's eighth ward, at the Locke-Ober
Cafe in 1898. Their man, Martin "The Mahatma" Lomasney,
was a sure bet to return to the state legislature—the fix was
in—and what better way to mark the occasion than with a
new cocktail?

Sometimes the inspiration for a cocktail was pure silliness.
A short-lived fad drink of the 1880s, the White Plush, came
into being, according to the *New York Herald*, when a dry-
goods buyer from New England went out for a night on the
town in Manhattan with two suppliers. Wary of being plied
with drink, he insisted on ordering milk and seltzer. Little did
he know that the bartender, under instructions from the suppliers, was spiking the drink with whiskey. As the evening
wore on, the milks kept coming, with whiskey assuming a
larger proportion and the seltzer disappearing entirely. At one
point, the buyer tipped over his glass, watched the white liquid
spread over the table, and murmured reflectively, "Gosh, it
looks like white plush, don't it?" Or so the story goes. Students
of barroom etymology, beware.

New York supplied a disproportionate number of new cocktails—or at least its bartenders bragged more loudly and more
journalists were around to hear them. But New Orleans, with a
mere fraction of New York's population, contributed mightily
to the development of the cocktail. Antoine Peychaud, mixing
up bitters at his apothecary shop—in a building still standing
at 437 Royal Street—may or may not have been the father of
the cocktail, but there is no doubt at all that New Orleans gave
birth to the Sazerac and the Ramos Gin Fizz. Both drinks are
solid classics, full equals of the old-fashioned and the mint
julep, yet they await rediscovery. The third drink associated
with the city, an absinthe frappé served at the Old Absinthe
House, is now but a folk memory.

The Sazerac was born at 13 Exchange Alley, in a bar owned
by John B. Schiller, the local agent for the brandies of Sazerac-
de-Forge et Fils in Angoulême. In 1859 Schiller opened his bar,
naming it the Sazerac Coffee House and prominently featuring
brandy cocktails. In time, rye or bourbon replaced the cognac
and a dash of absinthe was added for interest. When the law
decided that absinthe was a little too interesting, a local substitute was developed: herbsaint.

The fragrant Ramos Gin Fizz was born soon after Henry C.
Ramos arrived in New Orleans in 1888 and bought the Imperial Cabinet Saloon (he later moved to the Stag Saloon, opposite the St. Charles Hotel). The drink, a mixture of gin, lemon
juice, a few drops of orange-flower water, powdered sugar, egg
white, cream, and seltzer, depends on prolonged and vigorous
shaking to achieve the proper ethereal lightness. During Mardi
Gras, as many as thirty-five bartenders could be seen shaking
up fizzes at Ramos's establishment.

Lafcadio Hearn, the idiosyncratic New Orleans literary
critic, took a special interest in the food and drink of his native

city, going so far as to open his own restaurant, with everything on the menu priced at a nickel. The venture failed when his partner ran off with the cash, but in 1885 Hearn turned his culinary knowledge to account in *La Cuisine Créole*, which contains recipes and observations on the New Orleans way of drink. Although Hearn lists gin fizzes, absinthe drinks galore, and assorted juleps, punches, pousse-cafés, and "squirts," his heart belongs to the brûlot (which he calls a brûlé), a flaming after-dinner punch made with French brandy, kirsch, maraschino, cinnamon, and allspice. Hearn, whose imagination ran naturally to chiaroscuro, loved the ritual. The lights would be lowered, and a silver bowl would make its way to the center of the table, casting a spooky glow. There it was transferred to glasses in a ladle filled with brandy-soaked sugar cubes. A petit brûlé, for one person, was concocted in a hollowed-out orange half, the skin adding piquancy to the brew.

The only city to rival New Orleans was San Francisco, whose grand hotels of the gaslight era equaled the best that New York could offer. The city's better bars formed a chain

---

GRAND BRÛLÉ À LA BOULANGER.

[From a Gourmet.]

The crowning of a grand dinner is a brûlé. It is the *piece de résistance,* the grandest *pousse café* of all. After the coffee has been served, the lights are turned down or extinguished, brûlé is brought in and placed in the centre of the table upon a pedestal surrounded by flowers. A match is lighted, and after allowing the sulphur to burn entirely off is applied to the brandy, and as it burns it sheds its weird light upon the faces of the company, making them appear like ghouls in striking contrast to the gay surroundings. The stillness that follows gives an opportu-

known as the Cocktail Route, which began at the Reception Saloon on Sutter Street and wound its way to upper Market Street. The city's principal contribution to the mixed drink was Pisco Punch, also called Button Punch, invented at the Bank Exchange in the 1870s. Pisco brandy, a South American product, is distilled from the sweet muscat grape, and the best examples came from the Peruvian port city of Pisco. The New York journalist Thomas W. Knox wrote, "It is perfectly colorless, quite fragrant, very seductive, terribly strong, and has a flavor somewhat resembling Scotch whiskey, but much more delicate with a marked fruity taste." Knox described drinking it hot, with lemon and nutmeg.

Rudyard Kipling was treated to a sample—perhaps several samples—in 1899. The drink made an impression. "It is the highest and noblest product of the age," he wrote. "I have a theory it is compounded of cherub's wings, the glory of a tropical dawn, the red clouds of sunset, and the fragments of lost epics by dead masters." In other words, it went down easy.

---

nity for thoughts that break out in ripples of laughter which pave the way for the exhilaration that ensues.

Pour into a large silver bowl two wineglasses of best French brandy, one half wineglass of kirsh, the same of maraschino, and a small quantity of cinnamon and allspice. Put in about ten cubes of white sugar; do not crush them, but let them become saturated with the liquor. Remove the lumps of sugar, place in a ladle and cover with brandy. Ignite it as before directed, then lift it with the contents from the bowl, but do not mix. After it has burned about fifteen minutes serve in wine glasses. The above is for five persons, and should the company be larger add in proportion. Green tea and champagne are sometimes added.

—Lafcadio Hearn, *La Cuisine Créole* (1885)

It was long thought that the recipe for Pisco Punch died with Duncan Nicol, a Scot who managed the Bank Exchange from 1870 until Prohibition closed it down in 1920. Nicol was secretive about the punch. But in the 1960s an amateur historian tracked down the last bartender to work at the Bank, who divulged the recipe, a simple one with a little trick. The base ingredients were nothing more than Pisco brandy, lemon juice, and pineapple. The secret was to steep pineapple cubes in sugar syrup overnight.

With Prohibition, the golden age of the cocktail came to a dead stop. It was too good to last, and Americans seemed to recognize the fact. The saloon went out with barely a whimper: the night of January 16, 1920, saw a resigned, peaceful America drift quietly into a theoretically cocktail-free era. Wakes were held in cities throughout the land. Some bars gave out miniature coffins as souvenirs. At the Park Avenue Hotel in Manhattan, a casket was filled with black bottles. But the riotous send-off anticipated by the police never materialized.

The mood was one of regret and resignation. The great bars, the grand hotels, the splendid cocktails—all vanished overnight, as though whisked away by an incantation. "The Bamboo Cocktails at the Holland House," one writer lamented, so forlorn that he could only list his losses,

the Jack Roses at Eberlin's, the two for a quarter Manhattans at the Knickerbocker bar, the Thomas Flyers at Sherry's, the Infuriators at the Beaux Arts, the Orange Blossoms at the Manhattan, the Central Park Souths at the Plaza, the Absinthe Drips at Murray's, the Silver Fizzes at the Waldorf, the Perfect Cocktails at Delmonico's, the Old Fashioneds at the Imperial, the Mint

Juleps at the Astor, the Diamond Fizzes at the Belmont, the Rickeys at Captain Church's, the Clover Clubs at the Buckingham, the Bronxes at the Holland House, the mint drinks at the Green Turtle, the Gin Daisies at Rector's, the Whiskey Sours at Burns's . . .

It was all over, forever.

SEVEN

THE JAZZ AGE

Turkey Cocktail: To one large turkey add one gallon of vermouth and a demijohn of Angostura bitters. Shake.
                            —*The Notebooks of F. Scott Fitzgerald*

When William Powell first appears in *The Thin Man,* he's an anonymous figure off to the right of the screen, vigorously working a silver cocktail shaker near the bar of the Normandie Hotel. Gradually, the moving camera threads its way through the crowd, and Powell, playing detective Nick Charles, comes into full view. It turns out that while shaking, he is explaining the right way to mix a martini. "The important thing is the rhythm," he says, slurring his words slightly. "A Manhattan should be shaken to a fox-trot, the Bronx to a two-step, but a dry martini must always be shaken to a waltz. Mind you, there's a still more modern trend—" But the new trend remains a mystery.

Enter Nora Charles, fresh from Christmas shopping, pulled by Asta on a leash. Peeved at missing out on the drinks, she immediately orders five martinis. Cut to the Charles bedroom next morning: Nora recumbent with an ice bag on her head, as Nick and Asta look on sympathetically.

The Thin Man appeared in 1934, just after it again became legal for Americans to drink. But its ethos is soaked, so to speak, in the cocktail atmosphere of Prohibition, a pointless fourteen-year exercise that proved, at great expense to the taxpayer, the rather obvious truth that if citizens are deprived of legal liquor, they will seek out illegal liquor. Once Congress passed the Eighteenth Amendment and the Volstead Act, which put it into effect, the saloon immediately gave way to the speakeasy, sparking a revolution in taste and manners. To the sound of a thousand chattering cocktail shakers, women stepped right up to the brass rail and drank with the men. Gin was crowned king, and the fun began.

In the popular imagination the 1920s and the cocktail are synonymous. In fact, its greatest age had just ended, but its career as a symbol of modernity was only beginning. With Europe devastated and profoundly demoralized by war, a rich and confident America stepped into history's spotlight, impossibly glamorous, stylish, and above all, modern. As the stock market soared, it rushed full tilt into the age of the automobile and the skyscraper, while the great democratic cultural forms—the movie, the animated cartoon, the comic strip, jazz—achieved a state of perfection almost overnight. In industry and the arts, America radiated self-assurance and boundless energy. The nation was in a festive mood. And the cocktail was its totem.

The 1920s register in the imagination as a tempo as much as anything else. The cocktail shaker was a metronome for a decade in which everything was fast. It matched the speeded-up world of the newsreel and the silent film, the rapid steps of the Charleston, and the frantic arm-waving on the floor of the stock exchange.

Conventional wisdom has it that Prohibition did not work, that Americans drank more during the Jazz Age than ever before. This is not quite true. Overall, the country was drinking a little less by the time Prohibition limped toward the finish line, but the trend had been downward anyway. Those who did drink, however, drank more, and they gravitated toward hard liquor, the bootlegger's choice. Spirits were easier to make, more compact, and less detectable than beer or wine. Prohibition, in other words, turned a lot of beer and wine drinkers into gin and whiskey drinkers.

Prohibition not only changed what Americans drank, it also changed the way they drank. It put a nudge and a wink into the experience. It encouraged the massive binge, the hangover worn as a badge of honor, the barely hidden hip flask, proof that the owner belonged to a daring fraternity. Because a drink was denied by law, those who did drink were determined to do it up right when the opportunity arose. After penetrating the inner sanctum of a speakeasy, what was the point of sipping tentatively? Especially if you were in town for only a few days.

This was the era that coined the phrase "making whoopee." And whoopee required effort. It didn't make itself. Americans put a lot of work into their fun. Moreover, something in the air—the same mysterious ingredient that inspired flagpole sitting and goldfish swallowing—encouraged recklessness. "Take three chorus girls and three men," ran one facetious recipe from the 1920s, "soak in champagne till midnight, squeeze into an automobile. Add a dash of joy, and a drunken chauffeur. Shake well. Serve at 70 miles an hour. Chaser: a coroner's inquest."

Much of the heat in the battle between wets and dries was generated by moral friction between the city and the country.

From the vantage point of a Kansas farm, places like Chicago and St. Louis looked like moral cesspools. The Eighteenth Amendment helped turn myth into reality. In New York especially, Prohibition did not prohibit. "Back in 1920," F. Scott Fitzgerald wrote, "I shocked a rising young businessman by suggesting a cocktail before lunch. In 1929 there was liquor in half the downtown offices, and liquor in half the large buildings."

The transformation got under way literally overnight. In accordance with the Volstead Act, passed the previous year, Prohibition commenced at 12:01 a.m. on January 17, 1920. The next day, in Manhattan, the 50–50 Club opened over a garage at 129 West Fiftieth Street, launched by fifty members who paid one hundred dollars each for the privilege of keeping whiskey in lockers. There was no bar. The practice spread quickly, as placid members of the middle class began thinking and acting like insurgents.

For most Americans, it was a sneaking sort of revolt. More than ever, a man's home was his castle, a fortress to keep the influence of Prohibition at bay. In olden days, liquor stayed in the local saloon, far from the eyes of wife and children. If pressed, Dad did his drinking on the sly, stealing a nip from a pint bottle under the stairs. Now, as a practical matter, most drinking, and a fair amount of distilling, was done at home. Suddenly, mixing a mean cocktail became one of the manly arts, like carving the holiday turkey. This new development set off a boom in the bar-accoutrement industry. One magazine writer, strolling through a department store in the 1920s, noted that it sold thirty-five styles of cocktail glasses (a dozen of them in silver), fourteen different cocktail shakers, and eighteen kinds of hip flask. With glass and shaker in hand, customers could then turn to any of several companies that sold nonalcoholic Bronx, martini, and Manhattan cocktails. Instructions on the package pointedly warned users to be careful not to add alcohol, otherwise they would be in possession of an illegal cocktail. God forbid.

Deprived of their biggest source of income, hundreds of legitimate restaurants and night spots folded. Fine dining in America sank into a desperate decline that took decades to reverse. The Great White Way instantly lost its sparkle as, one by one, the grand hotels, the legendary bars, and the splendid restaurants shut their doors, and seekers of entertainment, if alcohol was involved, slunk into speakeasies for their fun. Louis Sobol, the Broadway columnist, bore bitter witness to the transformation. "Broadway faded into a street of cafeterias, electric shoe-shining stands, nut shoppes, physical culture demonstrators and five-cent dance halls," he wrote, "as the gates to an invisible paradise in the Fifties along Fifth and Park avenues sucked away the silk-hat and ermine crowd."

A few speakeasies really did live up to the romantic notion of whispered passwords, trap doors, false entrances, and unimaginable splendor within. "Some speak-easies are disguised behind florists' shops, or behind undertakers' coffins," an amazed French visitor wrote. "I know one, right in Broadway, which is entered through an imitation telephone box." Membership cards were more common than passwords, which tended to be no more complicated than "Joe sent me." But peepholes really did exist. "Key clubs" issued door keys to their regular customers. Jack and Charlie's, which later evolved into the "21" Club, introduced an ingenious bit of evasive technology. Its bar was outfitted with an emergency button that caused the liquor shelves to upend and send their contents hurtling down a shaft to the basement, leaving nothing but broken glass and a suspicious aroma. No one knows how many speakeasies there were in New York. Stanley Walker, the city editor of the *New York Tribune*, quoted estimates as high as 100,000 and as low as 800 in 1926. The New York City police put the figure at 9,000, which included cordial shops and all other places known to sell liquor.

The better nightclubs and speakeasies cast a kind of spell in the 1920s. They became inseparable from the overall atmosphere of fun—what Fitzgerald called "the general decision to be amused." Decades later, old speakeasy hands would intone the honor roll of bygone Manhattan night spots, beginning with Texas Guinan's and the Kit-Kat and winding up with the Marlborough House, the Hi Hat, the Ha-Ha Club, the Stork Club, and 21 West Fifty-second.

The bartender suffered a fatal blow, however, as Prohibition made his glorious profession a crime. "Into what strange vale he dissolved no one is able to say," Russel Crouse wrote. "It is as though he, too, were swallowed in that last great gulp" as America downed its last legal cocktail.

Some bartenders went into exile, plying their trade at the American bars that sprang up all over Europe. Back home, the more daring bartenders continued to work illegally; the rest retired or stepped sideways into legitimate work at hotels and restaurants, like the spectral bartender in Fitzgerald's story "The Rich Boy," who winds up chilling nonalcoholic champagne at the Plaza Hotel.

The easiest way to serve a drink was to pour it straight from the bottle. A safer alternative was the "set-up." Nervous speakeasy owners wanted the option, in case of a raid, of putting the bottles in the overcoat pockets of their customers. Then they could claim they were only serving set-ups—glasses, ice, and club soda or ginger ale. The set-up quickly became an institution. At many restaurants and clubs, the waiter would bring over a tray with ice, glasses, and White Rock soda and then turn away discreetly as customers reached for their bottles and poured. (It was considered bad form to leave a flask in plain sight on the table.) The soft-drink companies made no effort whatever to disguise the new market for their product. It was no longer kids with freckles who turned up in their advertisements. Instead, print campaigns showed tuxedoed young blades in nightclubs eyeing, with suspicious enthusiasm, the little bottles of ginger ale offered by a waiter in black tie.

The Eighteenth Amendment made for some interesting legal arguments. Early on, a bank president in Chicago found himself in the middle of a precedent-setting case when he was arrested for possession of a hip flask. The District Court was asked to decide whether his trousers were, legally, a vehicle and should therefore be seized and sold at auction like an automobile.

Prices rose. The standard had been two drinks for a quarter. At the Waldorf Bar, a cocktail had cost twenty cents. With Prohibition, the base price in speakeasies became forty to eighty cents and rose from there to three dollars in the more luxurious spots.

Manhattan seemed to have a monopoly on the swanky places. Before Prohibition, the city was already firmly established as the national capital of entertainment, fine dining, and sophisticated fun. Against the odds, the nightlife tradition lived on. While other towns made do with thrown-together speakeasies, or "blind pigs," Manhattan offered (along with plenty of clip joints and squalid dumps) palaces of fine food, music, and illicit drink, not all of it rye whiskey or gin poured over set-ups. In 1922, a bar serving mixed drinks, as opposed to pouring straight from the bottle, opened in a brownstone on Fortieth Street east of Fifth Avenue.

The top speakeasies, located in posh town houses, served food prepared by chefs from the great hotel dining rooms that had gone under. A top-of-the-line speak might boast two bars, a dance floor, Ping-Pong and backgammon rooms, lounges, an art gallery, and a band. "Dark and guarded doors opened into a spreading world of enchantment," Louis Sobol wrote, "a world of soft lights, seductive scents, silken music, adroit entertainment, smoke and laughter, of perfection of food and service, of wines and liquors of the first quality, all in a setting of gold and silver and brocade, velvet, iron, glass, and exotic woods."

The Park Avenue Club, designed by the Viennese modernist Joseph Urban, had an octagonal bar surrounded by floor-to-ceiling mirrors. Urban was in such high demand that he required $50,000 in cash—up front—to take on a speakeasy job. At the Merry-Go-Round on East Fifty-sixth Street, customers hopped onto plaster horses and took a little trip as the bar completed a circle every eleven minutes. At the Country Club on Park Avenue, patrons could play Ping-Pong or miniature golf. The Aquarium served theme drinks like the Goldfish—equal parts Goldwasser liqueur, gin, and French vermouth. "The kingfish is the lobster who runs up the largest check, even though he gets stewed to the gills," wrote a wisecracking journalist in *Manhattan*, a short-lived publication whose series "Behind the Brownstone Front" profiled one "giggle-water parlor" each week.

The top speakeasies made it easy to run up the bill. Customers could pay a dollar for cigarettes sold in abbreviated ten-packs, two dollars for a pitcher of water or a tiny bottle of club soda, ten dollars for a pint of whiskey, and twenty-five dollars for a bottle of champagne. The cover charge at Texas Guinan's ran twenty dollars and more.

The crème de la crème was the Marlborough House. Prospective clients were led into a sealed wooden vestibule, where they pressed a pearl button and presented their credentials. On the first floor, banquettes in silver leather ran the length of silver walls with scarlet wainscoting, the walls decorated in a pattern of white storks with scarlet beaks. In the cabaret room on the second floor, done in royal blue and copper, with a ceiling of hammered brass, torch singers crooned against a full orchestra, while "Egyptian" magicians entertained the crowd.

In their eagerness to snare the well-heeled customer, the best speakeasies spent lavishly on food and entertainment. The drinks were always an uncertain affair. But the pleasurable mix of cocktails, dinner, a floor show, and dancing proved durable, and the speakeasy of the 1920s, without missing a beat, became the nightclub of the 1930s, 1940s, and 1950s, just as the tony speakeasy crowd, once they had been forced out of their pre-Prohibition enclaves, coalesced into café society.

Women liked the new set-up. No speakeasy could afford to segregate by sex, so for once women got to go along, and it's fair to say that the speakeasy played no small part in the unraveling of Victorian manners and ideas in the 1920s. "The old days when father spent his evenings at Cassidy's bar with the rest of the boys are gone, and probably gone forever," wrote the journalist Elmer Davis. "Cassidy may still be in business at the old stand and father may still go down there of evenings, but since Prohibition, mother goes down with him." This feature of Prohibition lasted after repeal, and represents the one positive contribution of the Eighteenth Amendment. Women finally civilized the saloon, not by closing it down, but by walking right through the swinging doors and ordering a drink alongside the men.

Like most all-male institutions, the sawdust-strewn temple, with its spitoons and racy canvases, was an obstacle to social progress. It was, in truth, juvenile, a grown-up version of the backyard clubhouse with "No Girls Allowed" painted across the door. It reinforced a sexual apartheid that was already falling apart at the turn of the century, a victim of its own contradictions. Predictably, the men grumbled, but more perhaps out of a sense of duty than actual conviction. Don Marquis, in *Her Foot Is on the Brass Rail*, offered a comic lament for the old barroom, but the work lacks bite; the easy social mingling of the speakeasy, and the legal cocktail lounges that it later spawned, were too obviously an improvement on the old institution.

The liquor changed, and so did the drinks. America had been a whiskey-drinking nation, and throughout Prohibition it waged a doomed struggle to remain one. Canadian whiskey and Scotch flowed into the country by a thousand illegal channels, and plenty of legal whiskey relabeled "For Medicinal Purposes" somehow made its way from doctors' offices to the open market. None of it remained intact. One bottle of good whiskey would be stretched with homemade hooch to make four or five bottles. The days of drinking neat whiskey were over. "Rye and ginger" became so popular in the 1920s and 1930s that sales of ginger ale nearly doubled between 1920 and 1928. When Garbo spoke on-screen for the first time, in *Anna Christie* (1930), her lines were "Gimme a viskey, ginger ale on the side, and don't be stingy, baby."

"Everyone was drinking, or had just finished a drink, or was just about to take one," John O'Hara wrote of a country-club party in *Appointment in Samarra*:

> The drinks were rye and ginger ale, practically unanimously, except for a few highballs of applejack and White Rock or apple and ginger ale, or gin and ginger

ale. Only a few of the inner sanctum members were drinking Scotch. The liquor, that is, the rye, was all about the same: most people bought drug store rye on prescriptions (the physicians who were club members saved "scrips" for their patients), and cut it with alcohol and colored water. It was not poisonous, and it got you tight, which was all that was required of it and all that could be said for it.

Whiskey is a difficult flavor to counterfeit. The quickest and easiest spirit to produce was gin—a despised, low-rent spirit since the days of Hogarth—and lots of Americans learned how. The standard method was to add oil of juniper to a mixture of 40 percent alcohol, 60 percent water—*et voilà!* "The gin is aged," one bar book observed, "about the length of time it takes to get from the bathroom where it is made to the front porch where the cocktail is in progress." Gin was simple. Gin was quick. Once the down-and-outer's choice, it became the spirit of the age.

Drinks fell into two categories: quick and easy, for fast consumption, and thick and sweet, to disguise the poor quality of

---

No doubt much of our youthful drunkenness, especially our sick stomachs, was due to the poor quality of Prohibition liquor and to the strange combinations in which we drank it. At Mario's, Lionel's and my favorite drink was something called a Bullfrog, made of gin, apricot brandy, and grenadine. We alternated our Bullfrogs with Alexanders; these were made, I think, of brandy, crème de cacao, and heavy cream. Alexanders were liquid desserts but we drank them not only before dinner but through long evenings of conversation.

—Diana Trilling, *The Beginning of the Journey* (1993)

the base spirit. Prohibition unleashed a thousand alcoholic milk shakes that can curdle the blood even at a distance of seventy-five years. The most famous of these was the Alexander, a repulsive mixture of gin, crème de cacao, and cream, but there were others, like the Cowboy, Scotch and cream over ice.

Johnny Brooks, in *My 35 Years Behind Bars*, gave a fair idea of how the typical Prohibition bartender plied his trade. "I've invented a lot of mixed drinks in my time," he wrote. "Some of them are known all over the country now and have become standard drinks. And some of them are not so well known, probably because they're not such good drinks." Brooks turned vague when it came to those drinks "known all over the country," halfheartedly taking credit only for the Between the Sheets (equal parts brandy, Bacardi, Cointreau, and lemon juice) but expressing a willingness to back off if challenged. He staked his claim to history on something he called the Cubanola, which he shook up for the first time in 1925 while tending bar in Westchester County. "Someone came in," he wrote, "and ordered a Bacardi cocktail. The bootleg Bacardi we had wasn't the real stuff, and it was raw. I decided to doctor it up a bit." Desperately trying to cover up the rum, Brooks added grenadine, orange juice, pineapple juice, lemon juice, and, finally, egg white for eye appeal. There it was—the Cubanola, which no one has ordered or heard of since. And so it was with a thousand creations of the so-called cocktail age, a designation that makes sense only if quantity is the criterion.

For Americans who broke under the strain, there was always Havana. No sooner had Prohibition become a certainty than steamship companies began outfitting vessels for overnight Florida-to-Cuba service. One Newark bartender moved his entire saloon to Havana, right down to the bar stools. Americans who made the trip rediscovered the joys of rum, most of them at the Floridita bar on Montserrat Street, where the legendary Constantino poured the daiquiris that Hemingway would soon make famous.

The daiquiri was not a new drink. It had been created in the late nineteenth century and named for the village of the same name, located near Santiago—which happened to be the site of the Bacardi distillery. The inventor might well have been an American engineer named Jennings Cox, who managed the properties of the Spanish-American Iron Company and the Pennsylvania Steel Company in Cuba. According to Linda Wolfe, who tracked down Cox's granddaughter while researching *Cooking of the Caribbean Islands*, Cox received some important American guests in the summer of 1896 but found that he had run out of gin. Wary of serving straight rum, he added lime juice and sugar. This was the cocktail equivalent of "Watson, I hear you"—a stunning breakthrough, all the more wondrous for its simplicity.

Among the newspaper clippings that Cox's granddaughter saved is the testimonial of Admiral Lucius Johnson, who served in the Spanish-American War and had the good fortune to run into Cox and his daiquiris. Johnson and his men took the daiquiri recipe, along with a large supply of rum, back to the Army and Navy Club in Washington, an event commemorated by a brass plaque in the club's Daiquiri Lounge. With this foothold on the mainland, the daiquiri found its way into bars across the United States. And when Americans turned up in Havana during Prohibition, they knew what to ask for.

But Havana had more to offer than the daiquiri. Tourists were also ordering Presidentes (Bacardi and French vermouth with a dash of curaçao or grenadine) and Mary Pickfords (Bacardi and fresh pineapple juice with a dash of grenadine). But it was the daiquiri that reigned supreme, and over the decades it made El Floridita a close contender with Harry's New York Bar in Paris for the title of most famous bar in the world.

Hemingway, of course, had a lot to do with putting the Floridita on the map. The bar had existed in one form or another since 1820, when it was called La Piña de Plata—the Silver Pineapple. With a nod to the new political order, it became the Florida after the Spanish-American War, or, affectionately, El Floridita. But it was just another bar until Hemingway walked in and wrapped a large paw around a sugarless frozen daiquiri, the creation of Constantino Ribailagua, a Catalan who had begun working at El Floridita in 1914. In the 1930s and 1940s, Hemingway and the drink he called a Wild Daiquiri achieved a seamless unity. He often worked his way through about a dozen of these lime Slurpees, sometimes ordering doubles, which became known as Papa Dobles. A. E. Hotchner, Hemingway's friend and biographer, gives the recipe as two and a half jiggers of Bacardi White Label, the juice of two limes and half a grapefruit, and six drops of maraschino liqueur, blended with shaved ice in a mixer and served in large goblets.

Hemingway's barroom labors bore delicious literary fruit: the daiquiri's unforgettable cameo appearance in *Islands in the Stream*, the finest description of a drink to be found in American literature. Thomas Hudson, with a painter's eye, takes a good long look in his glass "at the clear part below the frappéed top." He likes what he sees: "It reminded him of the sea. The frappéed part of the drink was like the wake of a ship and the clear part was the way the water looked when the bow cut it when you were in shallow water over marl bottom. That was almost the exact color." You have to look at a lot of daiquiris very closely to extract an image like that.

Hemingway's massive presence brought publicity—not to

mention a whopping tab—to any bar. Understandably, any number of drinking establishments claimed his patronage, just as all eighteenth-century houses between Virginia and New York suggest a connection with George Washington. La Bodeguita del Medio hung a sign at the bar purporting to be a quote from the old man: "My daiquiri at the Floridita; my mojito at the Bodeguita." The endorsement lent cachet to the Mojito, a kind of rum mint julep, but the evidence that Hemingway ever set foot in the place seems a little shaky. There is no question about the Floridita, where Hemingway's favorite bar stool has been retired, like a hall-of-famer's baseball uniform.

The best of the Prohibition bars still echo faintly with old voices, recalling those heroic days when drinking a cocktail was an act of defiance, a blow struck for civilized values, the city man's rebuff to Bible Belt and Corn Belt tyranny. The state decreed that Americans would be virtuous. The rattling cocktail shakers at bars across the land said otherwise.

Not surprisingly, the Noble Experiment ended with a whimper. In the course of nearly fourteen years, America had spent an estimated $36 billion on bootleg liquor, and the government had not a penny of excise tax to show for it. With the United States in the depths of the Depression, the jobs and the money that a legalized drink industry would generate looked doubly attractive. Enforcement of Prohibition had become a bad joke. It was time to call it a day. Beer and wine became legal as of midnight, April 7, 1933. On December 5, the Eighteenth Amendment was repealed. The manufacture and consumption of beverage alcohol, including spirits, was once again legal in the United States. The cocktail was back in legitimate business.

EIGHT

RECONSTRUCTION

America today must unlearn all the follies she was taught in the name of Bacchus and must learn all over again what she has unlearned.
—Magnus Bredenbek, *What Shall We Drink?* (1934)

With the cocktail legal again, life became simpler. So did the drinks. The postrepeal *Gun Club Drink Book*, endorsing the "general return to reason" that eliminated most of the baroque drinks of the 1920s, laid down the new law concisely: "A real cocktail is short and snappy."

Esquire lost no time in clarifying the rules. Legal liquor had barely begun to flow when it published a roll call entitled "The Ten Best Cocktails of 1934." It's an instructive list. Some of the drinks were bona fide classics: the old-fashioned, the dry martini, the Ward 8, the daiquiri, the vermouth cassis, and the champagne cocktail. Others were newcomers: planter's punch, the old-fashioned Dutch (an old-fashioned made with genever, or Holland gin), and the Harvest Moon (applejack, lime juice, and orgeat). The tenth drink on the list, the vodka cocktail, resonates eerily. In 1934, virtually no one had ever heard of the tasteless, colorless spirit that today outsells all others in the United States. The recipe was innocuous—vodka mixed with sweet and dry vermouth, then garnished with lemon peel—but the vodka certainly was not.

While welcoming the top ten, *Esquire* waved good-bye to "the pansies"—the ten worst cocktails of the previous decade. They were the Bronx, the Alexander, the Pousse-Café, the Sweetheart, the Orange Blossom, the Pink Lady, the Clover Club, the Fluffy Ruffles, the Pom Pom, and the Cream Fizz. The names alone relegate most of these drinks to cocktail hell. But why the Bronx should have offended so many so deeply is puzzling. Bernard DeVoto singled it out for a literary pistol-whipping in the 1940s, writing that there was only one thing to be said in its favor: it was not as bad as the Orange Blossom (equal parts orange juice and gin). But George Jean Nathan had beaten him to the punch back in the 1920s. Prohibition, Nathan had argued, was a kind of divine punishment for the excesses of the golden age, when silly people did silly things to perfectly good drinks. Worst of all was the introduction of fruit juice. Mixing orange juice and gin, he wrote, was as bad as mixing prune juice with Pilsner. The Bronx deserved a place in the hall of shame with the Colonial, the Bunny Hug, the Clover Club, and the Cream Fizz, a sickly combination of gin and sweet cream.

G. Selmer Fougner, in his "Along the Wine Trail" column for the *New York Sun*, theorized plausibly that Prohibition killed the Bronx through overuse. Everyone had gin, everyone had orange juice, and by the 1930s everyone was sick of the combination. As late as the 1950s a *Time* reporter found it necessary to administer a few extra kicks to the Bronx's prostrate form, calling it "a desecration of the martini, a cheerless drink now well on its way to oblivion." The Bronx was the Bukharin of cocktails, denounced with unseemly enthusiasm as the Stalinist orthodoxy of the martini rigidified. It's too bad, because the Bronx deserves to be counted among the classics. It is a very good cocktail.

With the 1930s, America settled down. The overheated inventiveness of the Jazz Age cooled, the frantic rattling of the cocktail shaker gave way to the gentle clinking of ice cubes in a highball glass, and peace settled over the land. After sifting through the bar book of the old Waldorf, one writer found that only 11 of its 513 drinks had survived. America was not in the mood to freshen up the list.

Mencken considered this new conservatism a sign of mental health. "The same sound instinct that prompts the more enlightened minority of mankind to come in out of a thunderstorm," he wrote, "has also taught it to confine its day-in and day-out boozing to about a dozen standard varieties—the mar-

---

"What did you drink?" McGibboney persisted. Mr. Holliday glowed with sentimental recollection.

"There used to be," he said softly, "a drink called the Golden Slipper that slipped down with the greatest of ease. I loved that; and a Ramos Gin Fizz; and best of all the Clover Clubs they used to mix at the Lafayette, with a sprig of mint in the white froth above the pinkness . . ."

He paused, for they were staring at him without interest or comprehension. It came to him, then, that they were both young—at least ten years younger than he. To these young people, who had come to maturity in the age of Eighteenth-Amendment Scotch and had never known anything else, he must seem a senile graybeard croaking out personal recollections of the Mexican War.

—Elmer Davis, *Friends of Mr. Sweeney* (1925)

tini, the Manhattan, the daiquiri, the sidecar, the orange blossom, the Alexander, the Bronx, and a few others."

True enough, but the florid bartending style of the golden age, and the deluxe cocktails that went with it, made the equally reasonable assumption that people sometimes celebrate special occasions. In a festive mood, they might want to try something different, or, just as diners today put a chef to the test by ordering a special tasting menu, they might challenge the bartender to invent something new. By the 1930s, though, Americans were happy just to get decent liquor, and in any case, hard times were taking the frivolity out of America's drink culture. The novelty of novelty had worn off.

Every aspect of drinking became standardized. In the 1920s, America had revolutionized advertising techniques, and the newly liberated liquor companies could now put them into effect. With lavish print campaigns, the giant distilling companies were able to establish national brands in a matter of months—most of them unheard of before Prohibition. Local bourbons like Chicken Cock and Green River, or ryes like Sunnybrook and Susquehanna, disappeared, their places taken by newcomers like Seagram's Seven Crown, Crown Royal, and Four Roses. Picturesque local labels were bought up by the big companies and retired. Almost unnoticed, straight rye whiskey vanished from the American scene. Once dominant in the Northeast and Middle Atlantic states, it became the quaint taste of a dwindling population of old-timers. This was a severe loss, since the substitution of bourbon for rye has grossly distorted the flavor of dozens of cocktails, chief among them the Manhattan.

The distilling industry, after undergoing a drastic consolidation, was soon dominated by four giant companies. The cocktail followed suit. Its name, once legion, came to be identified with a mere handful of drinks. Most people settled for a highball (whiskey or gin on the rocks with soda), about the laziest cocktail in existence, with Scotch taking precedence over rye beginning in the mid-1930s. The slightly more adventurous Collins—a highball plus lemon and sugar—replaced all manner of fizzes, rickeys, and bucks.

Drinking became less interesting. One of the few cocktails that the decade invented was the multi-rum Zombie, a heat-seeking missile that, after enjoying a brief burst of popularity, managed to linger on and find a place in the permanent repertoire. Lucius Beebe, the famous bon vivant, said he first encountered the drink at Trader Vic's restaurant in California (Trader Vic himself credited Don the Beachcomber, a Los Angeles restaurateur) but traced the drink's popularity to the 1939 World's Fair in New York, where it was a signature cocktail at the Hurricane Bar. The distinction is a dubious one. At the opposite extreme was the splendid but not very original gin and tonic, made possible after Canada Dry developed a bottled quinine beverage.

The art of the cocktail, like any other art, always moves back and forth between simplicity and expressive, exuberant complexity; between classicism and romanticism. Periods of frenetic creativity, initially productive, end in excessive ornamentation and even decadence. The inevitable next step is a return to order, an insistence on the classical virtues of harmony and restraint. After repeal, the aesthetics of the cocktail became almost severe.

"There are only two cocktails," Bernard DeVoto declared. The first was "a slug of whiskey" over ice, perhaps with a splash of Angostura bitters, or a twist of orange or lemon peel. The second permissible drink was the martini, in a ratio of 3.7 to one. No olive. In other words, after a century and a half of inspired work, the cocktail had arrived where it had begun, with the frontiersman's bittered sling, plus the martini.

But the reaction was as extreme as the excesses of the 1920s. It is possible that once Americans were given the chance to mix real cocktails again, they had forgotten what the real stuff tasted like, or what a crack bartender could do with the right ingredients. If some gay blade from the 1890s did happen to be in the mood to relive the old days, not too many bartenders could accommodate him. Cecil Thompson, an English journalist, showed up at the Plaza Hotel in Manhattan the night of repeal and suffered bitter disappointment. There were precisely two drinks on offer. The staff did not know how to serve anything else.

The headwaiter, a holdover from the old days, knew better, but his knowledge was out of date. "This is a new world to me, sir," he told Thompson. "In the old days, I could, of course, mix a perfect champagne cocktail, or a Manhattan, or a dry martini. Any of those normal drinks. But these young people, sir. They have been asking me for TNTs, and Maidens' Blushes, and Death in the Afternoons."

The problem was not limited to drink. Prohibition and the Depression had virtually annihilated fine dining in America. The great gastronomic temples like Delmonico's and Maxim's quickly collapsed when alcohol became illegal. Their sophistication and European flair did not return for at least half a century. The creativity and professionalism of the grand gin palaces disappeared along with the twelve-course dinner.

A rather sad commentary on this loss is Patrick Gavin Duffy's *Official Mixer's Manual*, published in 1934. Duffy had worked at the Ashland House in Manhattan, where the bar did a booming business during intermission at the nearby Lyceum Theater. Duffy was a bartender of the old school—the *very* old school, circa 1890. In his photo portrait at the front of the book, he looks stiffly at the reader, attired in a heavy black suit and derby hat. The philosophy is just as fusty. "I cannot too much deplore the custom which has become prevalent of late of free and general conversation between bartenders and patrons," he wrote in his preface, sighing for the days when the men behind the bar knew their place and their trade, and starched white linen was mandatory. Close study of his recipe list shows that he strongly believed in another time-honored bartending tradition: recipe theft. A hefty percentage of the drinks in *The Official Mixer's Manual* come straight from *The Savoy Cocktail Book*.

Not surprisingly, Duffy looked askance at the innovations of the Prohibition era. "Although we include in this collection many of the Cocktail Creations of those hectic days, we caution barkeepers and others against adopting some of them for general use," he wrote. Indeed, Duffy marked with an asterisk those mixtures he disapproved of but felt he must include "as a matter of record and as a mirror in which future Americans may see the follies which the enactment of the 18th Amendment produced." His blacklist included the Barton Special (calvados, Scotch, and gin), the Cowboy, and the rather appealing Fascinator, apparently because it contained the dread absinthe along with French vermouth, gin, and mint.

Duffy (who claimed to have invented the highball in 1895) was a strict constructionist, insisting on a healthy respect for basic ingredients. He disapproved of cocktails that mixed together gin and any other spirit, or spirits plus sweeteners like cream or raspberry syrup. At the same time, Duffy's book reflects, perhaps more strikingly than any other drink book of the period, the enormous changes brought about by Prohibition. Nearly half his cocktails are based on gin.

America never developed a new cocktail culture to equal the one that Prohibition destroyed. Perhaps it never could have. The forces of modernization that swept over the country in the early twentieth century rendered obsolete bartenders like Duffy and the establishments in which they worked. The cocktail of old had been a complex, labor-intensive affair, as ornate and overstuffed, in many cases, as a Victorian parlor. The nineteenth-century bar books contain hundreds of recipes as extreme, demanding, and artificial as anything in Escoffier. Changing circumstances demanded a streamlining of the cocktail, the kind of imaginative simplification that nouvelle cuisine brought to French cooking in our own time.

But the sweep of events did not encourage the cocktail's evolution. The hopped-up metabolism of Prohibition almost guaranteed that a period of slowdown, even somnolence, would follow. After repeal, liquor advertisements tended to show their product enjoyed at leisure, in quiet, genteel settings—a highball at the nineteenth hole, perhaps, or in a library fitted out with a few hunting trophies. The protagonist of the one-page magazine drama was generally an older man of substance—an insurance executive, say. With the youth culture of the 1920s in full retreat, the idealized liquor consumer became a kind of mentor figure, wise in the ways of the world, demanding in matters of drink. Often he was surrounded by sycophants keen to show their enthusiasm for the old boy's favorite drink, usually a highball made with a father-figure sort of whiskey—an aged spirit that required an apprenticeship to appreciate.

The period of readjustment after Prohibition was made even more difficult because distillers had no stocks of liquor on hand, a double hardship when it came to whiskey, which requires aging. At the end of the 1934 fiscal year, 85 percent of the American whiskey inventory was less than a year old. Hence the sometimes preposterous emphasis on pedigree. Mount Vernon rye, for example, claimed that it was first distilled "on the General's own estate," and that the whiskey was still made according to Washington's original recipe. All distillers favored dark-brown bottles whose nubbly surface patterns suggested a cut-glass decanter. The best defense is a good offense. If you're selling young whiskey, don't just call it mature, call it ancient.

No sooner had the situation begun to right itself than war broke out. By late 1942, all distillers were making "cocktails for Hitler." Production shifted to industrial alcohol, used to make smokeless gunpowder and rubber tires. Except for three one-month "holidays" granted by the government, no new liquor was produced, except by a few rum and brandy facilities that could not easily be converted. Whiskey reserves plummeted.

More important, American men were now in uniform. Whatever its virtues, the military life does not promote appreciation of the fine points of connoisseurship. Servicemen took what they could get when they could get it. "Military drinkers," one newspaper columnist wrote, "have been known to swallow anything from hair tonic to V-bomb juice to pernicious mixtures of Calvados-schnapps-champagne-red wine-brandy-cider-and-beer." If the writer was exaggerating, it was not by much. In *The Thin Red Line*, James Jones's novel about combat in the South Pacific, soldiers strip the shelves of a field PX after word spreads that Barbasol shaving cream and Aqua Velva shaving lotion are on sale. The Aqua Velva is mixed with canned grapefruit juice to make a drink "rather like a Tom Collins."

The Aqua Velva Collins was a sophisticate among combat

cocktails. When aftershave or medical alcohol could not be found, the inventive soldier turned to local raw materials. The dried fruit that came with J and K rations could be soaked in water and transformed into jungle juice. A near cousin of jungle juice could be made by punching a hole in a coconut, adding a few teaspoons of sugar, and plugging up the hole. Several hours later the plug blew out, signaling the cocktail hour. The drink tasted like soap. In Polynesia and Micronesia, soldiers fermented the roots of the kava tree. "Night fighter" was the fermented sap of the nipa palm, and "tuba" was the fermented sap from the heart of a coconut tree—so called because the sap was drawn off with a tube. On PT boats, sailors simply quaffed torpedo alcohol.

Stateside, taste bowed to necessity. With whiskey and gin hard to come by, America once again began exploring the margins, looking to Cuba, Puerto Rico, and Mexico. Between 1941 and 1944, consumption of rum increased fourfold, and for the first time, Americans became acquainted with a strange Mexican spirit called tequila. The quintessential 1940s cocktail was the Cuba Libre—rum and Coca-Cola—a harmless invention that was helped along by the Andrews Sisters song of the same name. The tune came from Trinidad, where some fifty thousand American servicemen were stationed at a naval base—and drinking a far better rum than the stuff being unloaded on a captive American market.

With the end of the war, something like a return to normalcy set in—conservative normalcy. As part of a 1947 field report on U.S. drinking habits, *Life* magazine surveyed a Dallas club and found that 20 percent of the members were drinking beer, 33 percent highballs, 20 percent Manhattans or martinis, 13 percent whiskey sours, and 7 percent Tom Collinses—solid, conservative, establishment drinks, reflecting straight-down-the-middle taste. That was to be the postwar order. No funny business. Nothing suspicious or unsound.

The national taste was discovering the beauty of bland, reflected in the astonishing rise of lighter, milder blended whiskeys. Immediately after Prohibition, the public regarded anything described as "blended" with a wary eye. The word suggested adulteration or dilution, the hallmarks of bootleg whiskey. The distillers, with limited stocks, continued to push blends—essentially, straight whiskey stretched with grain alcohol—and eventually prevailed. In 1933 blends accounted for about a third of the market. But in taste tests conducted by Seagram's, nearly two-thirds of drinkers in the heart of straight-whiskey territory voted for blends. Seagram's acted on the evidence. By 1946, blends accounted for 90 percent of the market. As the whiskey reservoir began filling up again, straight whiskeys fought back, but they never again regained more than a third of the market, and by 1950 blended whiskeys were outselling them eight to one.

The victory of blended whiskey marks a turning point in American drinking tastes and in the marketing of liquor. For the first time, the long-term trend, still dominant, toward lighter, less flavorful drinks was identified by the distillers and seized upon with a vengeance. It spelled an end to regional preferences as a serious factor in American drinking habits. As the major distillers consolidated into behemoths, they created

---

Marlowe's drinking habits are much as you state. I don't think he prefers rye to bourbon, however. He will drink practically anything that is not sweet. Certain drinks, such as Pink Ladies, Honolulu cocktails and crème de menthe highballs, he would regard as an insult.
—Raymond Chandler, letter to D. J. Ibberson, April 19, 1951

and marketed national brands, least-common-denominator spirits geared to the mass taste.

By 1951, even *Business Week* felt compelled to comment on the blandness of the American palate. It noted with some alarm that advertising agencies were all promoting brands as "mild," "light," or "dry." Meanwhile, the top cocktails, in order, were the Scotch highball, the bourbon highball, and, just edging out the Manhattan, the martini.

Occasionally, creativity struck. But the more fanciful cocktails of the period reflect a strange, synthetic exoticism. Take the Mai Tai. The drink was invented by Victor Bergeron— "Trader Vic"—who earned a niche in American popular culture with his Polynesian restaurants. According to the Trader himself, he first mixed the drink in 1944, at his Oakland restaurant, when he decided that the world needed another rum drink. "I took down a bottle of 17-year-old rum," he recalled. "It was J. Wray Nephew from Jamaica—surprisingly golden in color, medium-bodied, but with the rich, pungent flavor particular to the Jamaican blends." He took fresh lime, curaçao, a dash of rock-candy syrup, and "a dollop of French orgeat for its subtle almond flavor." After shaking it up with ice, Vic poured it out for two friends visiting from Tahiti, who said, "*Mai tai—ro aé*," meaning "Out of this world—the best."

The enormous success of Trader Vic's restaurants remains one of the more fascinating chapters in American taste. It sheds light on a period that embraced blandness in food, drink, clothing, and even politics with a fervor that only fifteen tough years of depression and war can explain. Shattered nerves ached for suburban lawns, easy-listening music, lots of air-conditioning, and predictability.

But man must have diversion of sorts. That's where Trader Vic came in. A native of Oakland, he opened a restaurant called Hinky Dink's in 1934. The decor, heavy on the antlers and snowshoes, found favor with the public, and he prospered. But Hinky Dink's was just the beginning. Bergeron liked to travel and pick up ideas, especially in the cocktail line, and his wanderings took him to Cuba, where he developed a deep appreciation of good rum drinks. The turning point came during a field trip to Los Angeles, where he noticed a new kind of bar, typified by Don the Beachcomber. The interior was a South Sea island fantasy, with palm trees, leis, bamboo mats, and tropical plants. Patrons, adrift in a Polynesian revery, sipped rum drinks from hollowed-out pineapples.

Bergeron liked what he saw. He raced back to Oakland and turned Hinky Dink's into a little corner of the South Pacific. Out went the trophies, in came the South Sea masks, war clubs, giant clamshells, and tiki gods. Trader Vic created a myth, and a new name, to sell the fantasy. To a go-ahead, commercial society (the term "rat race" was just about to be born), he offered the dream of pure leisure, endless beaches, and permanent sunshine. For civilization and its discontents, he had the cure: savage drinks.

Perhaps returning servicemen were nostalgic for the South Pacific. Perhaps the Rodgers and Hammerstein musical stirred a national longing to drink out of coconuts. Whatever the reason, Trader Vic's caught on and spread from city to city. Imitations were rife. An extraordinary number of American restaurants seemed to be offering luaus and Hawaiian guitars. The concept and execution were bogus, and Bergeron admitted it. "You can't eat real Polynesian food," he once said. "It's the most horrible junk I've ever tasted." So diners feasted on a thoroughly Americanized version of a less than compelling cuisine—and loved it. The drinks were about as authentic as the dishes, concoctions like the White Witch, the Suffering

Bastard, and Dr. Funk of Tahiti. One drink, the Rangoon Ruby, deserves special mention. A mixture of vodka, lime, and cranberry juice, it resurfaced in the 1960s under the name Bog Fog and now enjoys widespread renown as the Cape Codder. All these drinks made the perfect accompaniment to dishes like Bongo Bongo Soup and Bah-Mee.

By the early 1960s the tropical fad was humming along with enough velocity for Hawaii to begin marketing okolehao, a traditional firewater distilled from the root of the ti plant, whose leaves are used to make grass skirts. The cocktail chosen to launch this suspect beverage was the Coke 'n' Oke. It did not catch on.

If history repeats itself as farce, the Polynesian craze suggests that farce can return as straight drama. The last of the tiki gods disappeared in the 1970s, and the pu-pu platter is no more. But in the 1990s young bartenders and students of American popular culture began taking a long second look at Trader Vic's. Hacking away at the fake Polynesian underbrush, they discovered some interesting drinks. The bartenders at Trader Vic's far-flung outposts often developed a masterful command of the idiom, and their use of unusual rums and exotic ingredients now seems farsighted. The one-world, inclusive spirit of contemporary bartending has pushed the cocktail in all sorts of interesting directions, and along all sorts of fascinating historical trails. As fate would have it, the footprints in the sand, on one beach at least, belong to Trader Vic.

NINE

VODKA ÜBER ALLES

"A small carafe of vodka, very cold," ordered Bond.
—Ian Fleming, *Casino Royale* (1953)

The fate of the postwar cocktail can be read as a cold war allegory. The sanitized version of middle-class life that defined the 1950s, or served as its official myth, influenced the nation's drinking habits as well. Social and political circumstances deeply hostile to eccentricity tamed its wayward creativity, and the appetite for novelty that had launched a thousand cocktails of the golden age and the Roaring Twenties disappeared. The man in the gray flannel suit drank a dry martini, a gin and tonic, a Scotch and soda—safe choices that put you in solidly with the right people.

The fervor with which Americans pledged allegiance to the narrowest possible interpretation of the American way of life reflected a deep apprehension about the future and a bristling defensiveness in the face of Communism's global advance. Here, too, the cocktail faithfully mirrored the political anguish of the time. With a twist. For just as the United States was preparing for an apocalyptic struggle against the Soviet Union and sharpening its vigilance against enemies within and without, the American way of drink was already succumbing to Russian influence. Its most cherished cocktails were being infiltrated—and falling, one by one, like so many dominoes—by vodka.

For most Americans, vodka first flashed on the cultural screen at the Yalta and Teheran conferences, where the obligatory toasts were offered to Allied victory. FDR shook up a few of his wretched olive-brine martinis for Stalin and his aides. Unimpressed by this capitalist achievement, the Russians hoisted their traditional vodka, neat. It had warmed them in the desperate hours of Stalingrad's defense; it had propelled them across the ravaged Ukraine and onward to Berlin. This was no ordinary spirit. It was Bolshevism in liquid form.

Few Americans had even heard of vodka. The ones who had seemed to think it was made from potatoes, when in fact it is nearly always distilled from grain. The first recipe calling for its use appeared in *The Savoy Cocktail Book* (1930), which lists a Blue Monday (vodka, Cointreau, and blue vegetable juice) and a Russian Cocktail (gin, vodka, and crème de cacao), with humorous instructions: "shake well, strain into a cocktail glass, and tossitoff quickski." But the book was British and therefore unlikely to have been read by Americans. Moreover the United States did not recognize the Soviet Union until 1933, so imports of Russian vodka stood at zero. Latvian or Polish vodka could be found in the ethnic neighborhoods of large cities, but to all intents and purposes, the spirit was a mystery.

In 1934, however, a Russian émigré named Rudolph Kunett (formerly Kunetchansky) approached the sons of the Russian distiller Pierre Smirnoff and bought the American rights to his name and distilling process. Then he started making vodka in Bethel, Connecticut. It was a small operation, producing a grand total of twenty cases a day. In 1939 a sharp-eyed executive from Heublein, John G. Martin, bought the entire business for $14,000.

The customers, as it happened, were all out west. Like so many American enthusiasms, vodka started out as a California fad and then spread gradually to the rest of the country. Prompted by the "Smirnoff Leaves You Breathless" campaign, Americans discovered three things about vodka: it mixes with anything, it doesn't have a heavy liquor taste or smell, and it looks light and clean. Folk wisdom maintained that it would not inflict a hangover.

Vodka also had a cocktail gimmick behind it. In 1946 John Martin ran into a friend who owned a Los Angeles restaurant called the Cock 'n' Bull. The owner, who was English, had been trying to push imported ginger beer at the bar, with no success. Martin saw an opportunity to promote Smirnoff. He invented the Moscow Mule: vodka, ginger beer, and half a lime, served in a copper mug.

For the first time an invented cocktail was being used as a marketing device. The advertising executive who steered Smirnoff's campaign called the Moscow Mule "a Trojan horse" whose purpose was to introduce vodka to America. Heublein's salesmen traveled from bar to bar, explaining the drink to bar managers and supplying Moscow Mule signs to be displayed on walls and mirrors. Legend has it that in 1947, Joan Crawford threw a party and decreed that only vodka and champagne should be served. Her guests decided that the new drink was chic, and began serving it at their parties too. A countertheory holds that the film community latched onto vodka because it allowed them to drink on the set and elude the sharp eyes (and noses) of studio spies.

Vodka was on its way. Slowly but surely it spread from Los Angeles to San Diego and San Francisco. Then it rolled east. "From a potable *rara avis*, in the same class as usquebaugh and arrack," the *New York Times* reported in 1947, "it has become standard equipment in bars and cocktail lounges throughout the country." Even the conservative Oak Bar at the Plaza Hotel latched onto the fad, serving a Volga cocktail (vodka, orange juice, lemon juice, and grenadine).

The real growth lay ahead, as vodka's ripple became a wave. From perhaps 40,000 cases in 1950, sales leaped to 1.1 million cases in 1954, then increased fourfold the following year, when the word "vodkatini" entered the language. In 1967 vodka eclipsed gin in popularity. Nine years later, overtaking whiskey, it became the leading spirit consumed in the United States. And so it remains today. Game, set, and match to the Russians.

Even James Bond, sworn enemy of the Soviet Union, drank vodka. In his lethal hands, it seemed less a drink than a bracing tonic, as refreshing as the high-impact showers that magically washed away the effects of a SMERSH-administered beating. Lean and clean, with harsh overtones, it was the perfect fuel for England's fine-tuned engine of espionage.

Ironically, even as the Russians were dominating the cocktail abroad, at home they were suffering humiliating defeat. The same nation that had developed the hydrogen bomb and *Sputnik* could not invent a drinkable cocktail. In 1954, with great fanfare, the Cocktail Hall opened its doors on Gorky Street in Moscow. It was designed to present the state of the art in Marxist-Leninist mixology, and it did. Only a Soviet fashion house could have created anything more appalling.

Tops on the menu was something called a Battering Ram: vodka and Armenian brandy, to which a depth charge of peach, plum, and apricot brandies was added. The Lighthouse was sweet "hunter's vodka," port, and a teaspoon of cherry jam. The Health Resort called for Georgian brandy, Chartreuse, madeira, and Soviet champagne, with a garnish of two dried prunes.

Despite its commercial success, vodka has contributed very little to the cocktail. Insidiously, it has slipped in and offered itself as a tasteless substitute for gin. The gin and tonic became the vodka tonic. The Orange Blossom became the Screwdriver. Only old-timers recall that the gimlet was once a gin drink. And sometime in the 1970s, the martini—yes, the martini—became a vodka drink for most Americans.

As the classics underwent a vodka conversion, the rising generation discovered that vodka served its purposes ideally. Teenagers consume alcohol with the goal of getting drunk. The fewer obstacles in the way, the better, and acquired taste is an obstacle. As it happens, vodka by legal definition is "without distinctive character, aroma, or taste." In other words, 86-proof nothing. With vodka, the cocktail shed all its complications overnight, becoming nothing more than a goosed-up fruit drink—Hawaiian punch with sting.

Vodka has given us the Bloody Mary, the antidote to many a hangover. That counts for something. Oddly enough, the origins of the drink are nearly as difficult to tease out as the martini's. The comedian George Jessel took credit for its invention, but his version seems to have been a prototype, nothing more than vodka and tomato juice, according to Fernand Petiot, a bartender at Harry's New York Bar in Paris in the 1920s. Petiot, who later made his way to the St. Regis Hotel in Manhattan, put his own spin on the drink, adding Worcestershire sauce, lemon juice, salt, and cayenne pepper, along with a celery stick for stirring. His invention, called the Red Snapper, went on to win fame and glory as the Bloody Mary.

Like a two-stage rocket, vodka continues to climb. The budget and midpriced brands have leveled off in recent years, but the so-called superpremium vodkas—the high-priced imports—soar ever upward, powered by some very shrewd marketing and image doctoring. In the 1970s Stolichnaya from the Soviet Union established the fact that richer consumers will pay more for the prestige of an import. This golden truth, familiar to the auto industry for some time and to the luxury trade for centuries, revolutionized the liquor industry. The big money was waiting at the top end of the market, where sales volumes might be small but profit margins were huge.

"Stoli on the rocks" became a status symbol at American bars. But then the Soviets stumbled. In 1983 they shot down a civilian plane, Korean Airlines flight 007, and overnight Stoli became an object of hatred. Absolut vodka, from neutral, peace-loving Sweden, stepped into the breach, unleashing an advertising campaign to win the Stoli customer. It ended up redefining the image of vodka.

Absolut used its advertising to make a style statement. The campaign, still going strong, presents visual and verbal puns based on the Absolut name. In the early days, artists like Andy Warhol and Keith Haring were enlisted to design ads with minimal text—"Absolut Warhol" and "Absolut Haring." An "Absolut Christmas" ad turned the Absolut bottle into a snow scene, manufactured so that magazine readers could turn the page upside down and set the snowflakes in motion.

With its precision-engineered name and minimalist bottle, Absolut embodied the myth of purity that is central to vodka's current appeal. The old Smirnoff "breathless" campaigns more or less came out and announced, "Look, we all want a drink in the middle of the day, but it's starting to look bad." Absolut never so much as hinted that the product was actually alcoholic. It made a compelling visual statement, with a bottle that looked like a fireplug designed by Mies van der Rohe. The name implied that here at last could be found vodka from which the final traces of imperfection had been purged. The product could go right on the shelf next to the designer spring waters and look perfectly at home. With Absolut, the age of the healthy cocktail began.

The image of vodka as a refresher, and the cocktail as a kind of sports drink, reached an apotheosis with the Cosmopolitan, one of the stranger success stories of the present day. The drink, a pleasant blend of vodka, cranberry juice, lime juice, and Cointreau, is a slightly wealthier relative of cranberry coolers like the Cape Codder. It first surfaced in the late 1980s, and unlike other fad cocktails, it has not only survived but prospered. More than a decade after first being sighted, it may well be the most universally ordered mixed drink in America, for reasons that one can only guess at. It looks attractive in a glass, with a pink neon glow. It bursts with agreeable fruit flavors. The key to its phenomenal success may, however, be the name. No one feels silly ordering it. At a time when classic cocktails command new respect, it sounds as though it might have a pedigree. And as a statement, "I am cosmopolitan" is hard to improve on. Like a well-written sitcom, it flatters its audience into believing they are a little more sophisticated and knowing than they really are. It's an insider's cocktail that absolutely everyone drinks, a glossy fake that with effortless charm has insinuated itself into the cocktail repertoire. Like the talented Mr. Ripley, it showed up one day wearing the right clothes. No one knows if it will ever leave.

TEN

THE COCKTAIL RESURGENT

America has invented, and always will invent, more of the
world's good mixed drinks than all the rest of humanity
lumped together.

> —Charles H. Baker, Jr.,
> *The Gentleman's Companion* (1939)

Where is the cocktail today? In a very good place. At last.

For nearly twenty years, journalists and drink writers have
tirelessly proclaimed the return of the cocktail, even when evidence was very thin that the cocktail had any intention of
showing up for an encore. It was a useful fiction. Magazines,
which depend heavily on advertising from liquor companies,
realized early on that it pays to be optimistic about the cocktail.
Inspired by the bottom line, editors commissioned article after
article on the martini, the Manhattan, the Sidecar, and all sorts
of glamorous drinks that no one really was drinking.

A true believer in classic cocktails, and in the possibility of
renewed creativity behind the bar, would have found the land-
scape bleak about fifteen years ago. Historically, the center of

gravity had shifted in the world of drink. In the past, when liquor companies were small and the advertising industry had not mastered the dark arts of mass persuasion, the cocktail's laboratory of invention was the local bar. Its chief scientist was the fellow with the handlebar mustache standing behind the mahogany; its consumer and judge was the man with his foot on the brass rail. But in the postwar era, the inspiration for new cocktails tended to come from liquor companies keen on boosting sales of a particular product.

In principle there's nothing wrong with industry-generated recipes. Who knows the product and its potential better than the people who make it, after all? But let us judge the results. In 1951, Seagram's tried to help sales of its Ancient Golden gin with a gin-and-grapefruit cocktail it dubbed the Seabreeze. It failed to catch on. The Moscow Mule may have succeeded in bringing vodka to the attention of America, but the mule has long since headed back to the barn. In 1960 the producers of Galliano liqueur launched something called the Golden Dream, with equally dismal results. Undeterred, Galliano struck again in 1970 with the Harvey Wallbanger—orange juice, vodka, and a dash of Galliano. This time, the company backed the cocktail with a large advertising campaign that featured a jolly little cartoon character named Harvey. The approach paid off, at first. Sales of the liqueur tripled in three years. But the drink, like all the other product-promoting cocktails, survived only as long as advertising supported it.

The same dynamic could be seen at work in the extraordinary peach schnapps bonanza of the mid-1980s. Peach schnapps was developed by a flavor scientist named Earl LaRoe, working for National Distillers, a company that was later bought by DeKuyper. Back in the early 1980s LaRoe and his colleagues at the flavor lab were hot on the trail of what

LaRoe called "the big, fresh-peach profile," with an eye to creating something exciting in the schnapps line. They succeeded beyond their wildest dreams. With virtually no advertising, Peachtree Schnapps became the first spirit since repeal to sell more than a million cases in its first year. Before long, nearly forty different brands of peach schnapps were on the market. In Iowa, peach schnapps outsold all other spirits.

This was a fad bordering on a frenzy. And at the center of it all was the idiotic Fuzzy Navel—peach schnapps, vodka, and orange juice. In the Midwest, where schnapps had always been popular, the Fuzzy Navel and its obnoxious cousins—the Silk Panties (peach schnapps and vodka), the Slippery Nipple (peppermint schnapps and Bailey's Irish Cream), and, most embarrassing of all, the Teeny Weeny Woo Woo (peach schnapps, vodka, and cranberry juice)—became a kind of cult, rallying points for young drinkers in search of fun and not too picky about taste. Eager to cash in, the distillers released a tidal wave of flavored schnapps: pear, strawberry, even root beer. But the sort of drinker who would step up to the bar and order a Teeny Weeny Woo Woo with a straight face turned out to be unreliable.

Flavored schnapps enjoyed its fifteen minutes of fame, and then American youth stampeded to the next attraction. The schnapps audience quickly embraced such delights as the Screaming Orgasm (Grand Marnier, Kahlua, and Bailey's Irish Cream) and the Jell-O Shot consumed from a little paper cup. Devotees called this "sucking slime." At the more ambitious drink palaces, bartenders carved serpentine grooves into a big block of ice, creating ski runs for their Jell-O Shots. The colored blobs would speed down the ice and into the mouth of a waiting customer. One of the cleverest of the Jell-O drinks was something called the Lava Lamp, a long drink of vodka and soda with chunks of Jell-O floating in it. The French, bless their hearts, created their own version, dead ringers for fruit jellies, served on a square Japanese plate with chopsticks.

Meanwhile, virtually every magazine that paid attention to cocktails held fast to the vision of smart young things sipping icy cold martinis in a deco lounge. Out in the real world, the cocktail seemed to be entering terminal decline. Bartenders were serving frozen margaritas from a hose gun. New Orleans Original Daiquiries, a chain operation, developed prefab frozen drinks like the Triple Bypass, the Dreamsicle, and the Bubble Gum. Their relationship to the daiquiri was unclear. One company executive explained that the American public now considered any frozen drink other than a margarita to be a daiquiri.

This downward slide looked as if it might even take the bartender with it. A company called Honeybee Robotics created Robotender, a mechanical barman with a video monitor for a head. It could shake more than a hundred different drinks. It could tell jokes. It could tune itself out and show music videos.

Just when the cocktail cause seemed hopeless, the winds of change began to blow—softly at first, then with increasing force. The restless rediscovery of past American styles came to the rescue. A fascination with Hollywood films of the 1940s and 1950s, and with jazz singing from the same period, coalesced in lounge culture and the swinging lifestyle of the Vegas Rat Pack. Drinking—a specific kind of drinking—was central to the swinging image, and frozen daiquiris were definitely not part of it. The martini was the lifeblood of lounge, and suddenly, after years of futile promotion by desperate journalists, young people could be seen sipping drinks with olives in them. The classic cocktail was back—fashionably late, but undeniably fashionable.

Nostalgia for old-style Hollywood glamour dovetailed with powerful new currents on the culinary scene. In cities all over the United States, bartenders began looking into old bar books and rediscovering long-forgotten cocktails. With the same sense of mission that was leading young chefs to seek out pristine ingredients at local markets, they began insisting that their fruit juices be freshly squeezed. Out went the powdered sour mixes. The discovery of Caribbean rums and flavorings, Mexican tequilas, and South American drinks like cachaça and Pisco brandy opened up new avenues of invention. Dissatisfied with commercial products, especially flavored vodkas, many bartenders began infusing their own liquors with fruits and herbs.

Chefs began to look on cocktails as an extension of their food menus. Productive collaborations developed between bartenders and chefs. New ingredients and flavors entered the repertoire, as the herbs and spices of fusion cooking made their way into the cocktail glass, with startling results. At Sono, a Japanese-influenced fusion restaurant in New York, the house drink is a margarita accented with shiso, a fragrant oriental leaf whose flavor lies somewhere between basil and mint. At Tabla, a New York restaurant with an Indian bent, the cocktails converse with the menu, incorporating spices like cardamom and turmeric.

Culinary enthusiasms like these have reinvigorated the cocktail and expanded the flavor spectrum. For the first time in a long time, the cocktail looks as though it has a future—an exciting future. There are probably more innovative bartenders at work today than there have been in generations. They have an appreciative audience that places a premium on stylish drinking. It is commonplace now to enter a good bar or restaurant and see a card on the table listing special cocktails, or to find a cocktail section on the menu. Back in the 1970s, a prescient bartender warned an inquiring magazine writer not to give up on the martini. The same young drinkers who scorned it now would find their way back to it. He was right. What he failed to see was the powerful spell it would cast, along with the other great cocktails of the golden age, over the twilight years of the twentieth century. The new millennium has barely begun to take its first, halting steps, but for the cocktail the immediate future looks very bright. More than a century after the martini and the Manhattan conquered the world, the American mixed drink looks poised to enter its second golden age.

RECIPES

The 103 recipes in this section reflect my own biases and tastes. The list is not encyclopedic. I don't see the point in offering, as a bartenders' manual must, hundreds of recipes, most of which are undrinkable. Instead, I have sifted and winnowed, trimmed and pared, aiming for a lineup that includes the great classics, revives some worthy but forgotten favorites of days gone by, and finds room for promising newcomers.

If the group seems heavy on champagne cocktails, that's because they kick off a social occasion with great flair, and most hosts are more willing to mix fancy cocktails at the beginning of the evening than at the end. I can't think of a better use for so-so sparkling wine, and I have never seen anyone fail to perk up at the sight of a tray of champagne cocktails. Straight rye whiskey also shows up in several recipes. If it seems exotic, remember that most of the whiskey cocktails of the nineteenth century were formulated with rye in mind, and modern taste, which places a premium on dryness, should delight in rediscovering this great spirit, which is making a bit of a comeback. A few years ago, there were only three straight ryes on the market: Old Overholt, Wild Turkey, and Jim Beam. Now several other distilleries make straight rye in small batches, which means the Manhattan may have a fighting chance to show why it was once the king of cocktails.

The reader should note with some relief that any modest bar will be equipped to make the cocktails on my list. Anyone starting from scratch can work up to fighting strength by buying a bottle each of bourbon, rye, blended Scotch, white rum, amber rum, cognac, gin, applejack, vodka, sweet vermouth, dry vermouth, tequila, Campari, Angostura bitters, Cointreau, tonic, and soda. Stick to high-quality spirits. The better the materials, the better the drink, up to a point. Inexpensive champagne makes a better champagne cocktail than a cheap Spanish cava, but it would be foolish to turn good champagne into a mixed drink. Do not pour serious cognac into your Sidecars. But bottom-of-the-line bourbons and Scotches can ruin a cocktail.

The hardware should include a cocktail shaker, a cocktail strainer, a long-handled stirrer, and a jigger. The so-called jigger is actually two metal measuring cups joined bottom to bottom. The larger one holds an ounce and a half of liquid and is known as a jigger. The smaller one, known as a pony, holds an ounce. Since fruit juices should be squeezed from fresh fruit, a sturdy manual juicer is good to have, although the bare hand works fine. (Mechanical juicers tend to throw pulp and rind into the drink.) When a cocktail requires a twist of the rind, use a razor-sharp vegetable peeler. The idea is to shave off an oil-filled sliver of outer rind, with no trace of the bitter white inner rind. Ambitious mixers might want to try the following trick. Cut a thick slice of rind (this time it's not only all right but necessary to have a lot of pith, since the point is to get a good grip on the peel). Squeeze the twist, skin side down, over a lit match held about six inches above the drink. The volatile oils in the skin will ignite in spectacular fashion, laying down a delicate slick of burnt lemon, lime, or orange over the drink surface.

Too much psychic distress has been caused by the shaken-versus-stirred controversy. Liquors do not bruise, so there's no point in being squeamish with them. But shaking will ruin an effervescent drink—that is, one containing champagne, soda, or tonic. And it will overly aerate tomato juice. Anything else can be shaken, and in fact shaking is the best method of getting a cocktail as cold as possible as quickly as possible. Crushed or cracked ice is ideal.

The quest for maximum coldness involves a trade-off. Ice lowers the temperature of the drink, but it melts, diluting the final product. There are three ways to minimize this effect. The first is to keep cocktail glasses and shakers in the freezer. The second is to use small cocktail glasses, which, if you look closely at old Hollywood films, was standard practice in the 1930s and 1940s. (One old bar book even insists that a cocktail should be no bigger than two ounces.) The third is to avoid serving cocktails on the rocks. Long drinks require ice in the glass, of course, but short drinks do not. Ice keeps them colder, but the drink turns soupy and the flavors become muddled. I prefer to shake and strain, and have so indicated in the directions to the cocktails in this section. But this is purely a personal matter.

Finally, every bar should have a bottle of simple syrup to sweeten drinks. Granulated sugar settles in the bottom of a glass, while simple syrup remains in solution. It is easy to make a batch. Heat equal parts sugar and water in a saucepan (say two cups each for a reasonable batch) over a medium-high flame until the sugar dissolves and the liquid becomes clear, about five minutes. Do not allow the mixture to turn brown. Let cool and store in a bottle with a pour spout. It will keep for several weeks. One teaspoon sugar equals two dashes of simple syrup.

Drinks marked with an asterisk are discussed in detail in the text.

WHISKEY COCKTAILS

AFFINITY

2 ounces Scotch
½ ounce French (dry) vermouth
½ ounce Italian (sweet) vermouth
1 dash Angostura bitters

Pour ingredients into an ice-filled shaker. Shake, then strain into a cocktail glass.

ALGONQUIN

2 ounces straight rye
1 ounce French (dry) vermouth
1 ounce pineapple juice

Pour ingredients into an ice-filled shaker. Shake, then strain into a cocktail glass.

APPROVE

Adapted from *The Savoy Cocktail Book* (1930)

3 ounces straight rye
2 dashes Angostura bitters
2 dashes Cointreau
Twist of lemon
Twist of orange

Pour liquid ingredients into an ice-filled shaker. Shake, then strain into a cocktail glass. Squeeze lemon and orange twists over the drink and discard them.

BARBARY COAST

From G. Selmer Fougner's "Along the Wine Trail" column in the *New York Sun* (1934)

2 ounces straight rye
½ ounce Italian (sweet) vermouth
½ ounce orange juice

Pour ingredients into an ice-filled shaker. Shake, then strain into a cocktail glass.

BROOKLYN

As David A. Embury pointed out in *The Fine Art of Mixing Drinks* (1948), the Brooklyn is simply a dry Manhattan with a dash of maraschino added, and the bitter element provided by Amer Picon, the French aperitif.

Adapted from *The Savoy Cocktail Book* (1930)

2 ounces straight rye
1 ounce French (dry) vermouth
1 dash Amer Picon (or 1 dash Angostura bitters)
1 dash maraschino liqueur

Pour ingredients into an ice-filled shaker. Shake, then strain into a cocktail glass.

LEMON PUNCH

Adapted from *The National Cookery Book* (1826)

1 quart whiskey
2 pounds sugar
12 lemons

Pare the rind from the lemons, making sure not to include the bitter white pith. Set the lemons aside. Boil the rinds in a gallon of water until the flavor is extracted, about 20 minutes. Squeeze the lemons and pour the juice over the sugar. Add the sweetened juice to the lemon water. Stir in the whiskey and bottle the punch.

MANHATTAN*

Like the martini, the Manhattan can be mixed sweet, semidry, or dry. The following recipe yields a semidry Manhattan. Use French vermouth only, and the drink is dry. Use Italian vermouth and the drink is sweet.

1½ ounces straight rye (preferably) or bourbon
¼ ounce French (dry) vermouth
¼ ounce Italian (sweet) vermouth
1 dash Angostura bitters
1 maraschino cherry (optional)

Pour liquid ingredients into an ice-filled shaker. Shake, then strain into a cocktail glass. Garnish with the cherry.

MINT JULEP*

From the Willard Hotel, Washington, D.C.

12 mint leaves (red-stemmed if possible)
1 teaspoon sugar
2 ounces bourbon
Carbonated water
1 sprig of mint
Lemon zest
Powdered sugar

In a tall crystal tumbler, gently bruise the mint leaves and muddle with sugar and a dash of bourbon. Fill the glass halfway with cracked ice and agitate with a spoon. Pack the rest of the glass with ice and fill with the rest of the bourbon and equal parts fresh water and carbonated water. Garnish with mint sprig. Twist a lemon zest over the leaves and dust with powdered sugar. Serve with two short straws.

NEW YORKER

From *The Stork Club Bar Book* (1946)

2 ounces straight rye
Juice of ½ lime
1 dash grenadine
Twist of lemon

Pour liquid ingredients into an ice-filled shaker. Shake, then strain into a cocktail glass. Garnish with the lemon twist.

OLD-FASHIONED*

The invention of the old-fashioned—an abbreviated name for "old-fashioned whiskey cocktail"—has often been credited to the Pendennis Club in Louisville, Kentucky. According to legend, Colonel James E. Pepper, a noted bourbon distiller, brought the recipe east when he traveled on business. The actual facts remain to be discovered. There's no question, though, that the old-fashioned is one of the oldest American cocktails, and one of the best. Unfortunately, at some point carbonated water made its way into the recipe. It should not be used.

2–3 ounces bourbon
1 dash Angostura bitters
1 cube sugar (or 1 dash simple syrup)
Twist of lemon
1 maraschino cherry (optional)

In the bottom of an old-fashioned glass, muddle the sugar cube with a few drops of water and a dash of Angostura bitters (or mix a dash of simple syrup and the bitters). Add bourbon and ice cubes. Garnish with the lemon twist and, if desired, a maraschino cherry.

POLICE GAZETTE COCKTAIL

From *The New Police Gazette Bartenders Guide* (1901)

3 ounces whiskey
2 dashes French (dry) vermouth
3 dashes simple syrup
2 dashes Angostura bitters
2 dashes curaçao
2 dashes maraschino liqueur
1 maraschino cherry

Pour liquid ingredients into an ice-filled shaker. Shake, then strain into a cocktail glass. Garnish with the cherry.

REMSEN COOLER

The name for this summer thirst-quencher comes from a now-forgotten brand of whiskey.

½ teaspoon superfine sugar (or 1 dash simple syrup)
4 ounces club soda
2–3 ounces Scotch or gin
Twist of lemon

In a Collins glass, dissolve the sugar in a dash of club soda. Add ice, Scotch (or gin), and stir. Top up with club soda. Garnish with the lemon twist.

ROB ROY

1½ ounces Scotch
1½ ounces Italian (sweet) vermouth
2 dashes Angostura bitters
Twist of lemon

Pour liquid ingredients into an ice-filled shaker. Shake, then strain into a cocktail glass. Garnish with the lemon twist.

ROYAL

It is important to use ginger beer, which has a hot spark to it, and not ginger ale, which is insipid and too sweet.

From Lafcadio Hearn, *La Cuisine Créole* (1885)

3 ounces whiskey or brandy
2 tablespoons ginger beer
1 teaspoon sugar (or 1 dash simple syrup)
1 dash Angostura bitters
Twist of lemon

Pour liquid ingredients into an ice-filled shaker. Shake, then strain into a cocktail glass. Garnish with the lemon twist.

SAZERAC*

In his *Famous New Orleans Drinks and How to Mix 'Em* (1937), Stanley Clisby Arthur gives the following recipe for the Sazerac, as mixed by Leon Dupont, a bartender at the Sazerac House. Most modern recipes call for bourbon instead of rye, and only one bitters, Peychaud's, which has a characteristic licorice taste. Herbsaint is a New Orleans pastis.

1 cube sugar
3 drops Peychaud's bitters
1 dash Angostura bitters
1½ ounces straight rye
1 dash absinthe substitute (a pastis like Pernod, Ricard, or Herbsaint)
Twist of lemon

Fill an old-fashioned glass with ice and let chill. In a second old-fashioned glass place a cube of sugar and add just enough water to moisten. Crush the saturated sugar with a bar spoon. Add a few drops Peychaud's bitters, a dash of Angostura, and rye. Add several lumps of ice and stir. Empty the first glass of its ice, add several drops of pastis, twirl the glass to coat the sides, and pour out any excess liquid. Into this glass strain the whiskey mixture, then twist the lemon peel over it.

WARD 8 *

1½ ounces straight rye (or bourbon)
½ ounce orange juice
½ ounce lemon juice
3 dashes grenadine

Pour ingredients into an ice-filled shaker. Shake, then strain into a cocktail glass.

WHISKEY COLLINS

2 ounces straight rye (or bourbon)
Juice of ½ a lemon
1 teaspoon powdered sugar (or 1 dash simple syrup)
4 ounces club soda

Pour the rye (or bourbon), lemon juice, and sugar (or simple syrup) into an ice-filled Collins glass. Top up with club soda and stir.

WHISKEY SOUR

1½ ounces straight rye (or bourbon)
½ ounce lemon juice
½ ounce lime juice
1 teaspoon powdered sugar (or 1 dash simple syrup)

Pour ingredients into an ice-filled shaker. Shake, then strain into a cocktail glass.

BRANDY COCKTAILS

ARMAGNAC LILLI

1 ounce armagnac
4 ounces blond Lillet
Orange twist or wedge

Pour liquid ingredients over shaved ice into a champagne flute. Garnish with the orange twist or wedge.

CALVADOS

2 ounces calvados
2 ounces orange juice
1 dash Cointreau
Twist of orange

Pour liquid ingredients into an ice-filled shaker. Shake, then strain into a cocktail glass. Garnish with the orange twist.

JACK ROSE

Jack Rose was a gangster who turned state's evidence in a notorious Manhattan murder case, the 1912 gangland slaying of a gambling-house operator named Herman Rosenthal. But common sense suggests that the name really refers to the drink's color and its main ingredient, applejack.

1½ ounces applejack
Juice of 1 lime
½ ounce grenadine

Pour ingredients into an ice-filled shaker. Shake, then strain into a cocktail glass.

NICKY FINN

From El Borracho restaurant, Manhattan, 1946. The name comes from the owner, Nicky Quattrociocchi.

1 ounce brandy
1 ounce Cointreau
1 ounce lemon juice
1 dash Pernod

Pour ingredients into an ice-filled shaker. Shake, then strain into a cocktail glass.

SAVOY STAR

Adapted from *The Savoy Cocktail Book* (1930)

1½ ounces calvados or applejack
1½ ounces gin
1 dash French (dry) vermouth
1 dash Italian (sweet) vermouth
1 teaspoon grapefruit juice

Pour ingredients into an ice-filled shaker. Shake, then strain into a cocktail glass.

SIDECAR

This is the one classic to emerge from the Prohibition era. Harry's New York Bar in Paris claims the honor of inventing it in 1931, but the drink flows freely in Carl Van Vechten's *Parties*, a collection of stories written in 1930. David A. Embury, in *The Fine Art of Mixing Drinks* (1948), says the drink was invented during the First World War by a friend of his, an Army captain who was driven to his favorite Paris bistro in a motorcycle sidecar. Inexplicably, the *American Mercury*, in a 1933 article, refers to it as "a ladies' drink," which is absurd.

1 ounce brandy
Juice of ½ lemon
½ ounce Cointreau

Pour ingredients into an ice-filled shaker. Shake, then strain into a cocktail glass.

STAR

Said to have been created at the Plaza Hotel in Manhattan in 1911, the Star cocktail was famous enough by the teens to be celebrated by Franklin P. Adams in his "Conning Tower" column in the *New York Tribune*.

1½ ounces applejack
1½ ounces Italian (sweet) vermouth

Pour ingredients into an ice-filled shaker. Shake, then strain into a cocktail glass.

GIN COCKTAILS

ABBEY

2 ounces gin
1 ounce orange juice
1 ounce blond Lillet
1 dash Angostura bitters
1 maraschino cherry

Pour liquid ingredients into an ice-filled shaker. Shake, then strain into a cocktail glass. Garnish with the cherry.

AVIATION

2 ounces gin
1 ounce lemon juice
2 dashes maraschino liqueur

Pour ingredients into an ice-filled shaker. Shake, then strain into a cocktail glass.

BARON

Martini recipes used to call for orange bitters, an ingredient almost impossible to find today. The Baron gives a faint idea of what the original must have tasted like.

2 ounces gin
1 ounce French (dry) vermouth
2 dashes Italian (sweet) vermouth
6 dashes Cointreau
Twist of lemon

Pour liquid ingredients into an ice-filled shaker. Shake, then strain into a cocktail glass. Garnish with the lemon twist.

BEAUTY SPOT

2 ounces gin
1 ounce grenadine
White of one egg

Pour ingredients into an ice-filled shaker. Shake, then strain into a cocktail glass.

BRONX*

1½ ounces gin
½ ounce French (dry) vermouth
½ ounce Italian (sweet) vermouth
Juice of ¼ orange

Pour ingredients into an ice-filled shaker. Shake, then strain into a cocktail glass.

BRONX TERRACE

2 ounces gin
1 ounce French (dry) vermouth
Juice of ½ lime
1 maraschino cherry

Pour liquid ingredients into an ice-filled shaker. Shake, then strain into a cocktail glass. Garnish with the cherry.

CAMPDEN

2 ounces gin
1 ounce Cointreau
1 ounce blond Lillet

Pour ingredients into an ice-filled shaker. Shake, then strain into a cocktail glass.

CITY BREEZE

1 ounce gin
2 ounces Pimm's No. 1 Cup
3 ounces lemon ginger tea (recipe follows)

Pour ingredients into an ice-filled shaker. Shake, then strain into a cocktail glass.

LEMON GINGER TEA
1 quart water
1 lemon
¼ cup freshly grated ginger
¼ cup honey

Bring the water to a boil. Add the juice from the lemon, the squeezed lemon, and the ginger. Turn off the fire. Let steep for 20 minutes. Stir in the honey and strain. Use for City Breeze, or serve as a nonalcoholic drink over ice with thin slices of lemon or lime. Can also be served hot with a cinnamon stick.

DEPTH CHARGE

2 ounces gin
2 ounces blond Lillet
2 dashes Pernod
Twist of orange

Pour liquid ingredients into an ice-filled shaker. Shake, then strain into a cocktail glass. Squeeze the orange twist over the drink.

FLAME OF LOVE

From Chasen's Restaurant, Hollywood

Scant teaspoon dry (fino) sherry
2 thick slices of orange peel
1–2 ounces gin or vodka

In a chilled martini glass, swirl the sherry to coat the sides, then pour off any excess. Pass the orange peel over the flame of a match held over the glass, squeezing the peel, skin side down. The oil in the peel should ignite, depositing a burnt orange mist in the glass. Discard the peel. Fill the glass with ice and add the gin or vodka. Stir. With the second slice of orange peel, repeat the first step. Discard the peel. Serve.

FRENCH 75

The name of this old favorite refers to a piece of French artillery used in the First World War. The drink was originally compounded of cognac, lime or lemon juice, and simple syrup. Somewhere along the way it underwent a metamorphosis.

$1\frac{1}{2}$ ounces gin
Juice of $\frac{1}{2}$ lemon
$\frac{1}{2}$ teaspoon powdered sugar
4 ounces chilled champagne
Twist of lemon

Mix the gin, lemon juice, and sugar in a Collins glass half-filled with crushed ice. Top up with the champagne. Garnish with the lemon twist.

GIMLET

The gimlet started out as a lime rickey without the carbonated water. When vodka appeared on the scene, the gin gimlet faded from the scene, and even a tough guy like Raymond Chandler's Philip Marlowe made the trendy switch. He also drank his gimlets very sweet, half vodka and half Rose's.

2 ounces gin (or vodka)
$\frac{1}{4}$ ounce Rose's lime juice
Twist of lime

Pour liquid ingredients into an ice-filled shaker. Shake, then strain into a cocktail glass. Garnish with the lime twist.

GIN BUCK

The Gin Buck was one of the more popular Prohibition drinks, for obvious reasons. It was easy to make, and ginger ale, in addition to sweetening the drink, helped smooth over rough spots in the gin.

¼ lemon
3 ounces gin
4 ounces ginger ale

Squeeze the lemon into a highball glass, add cracked ice and gin, and stir. Add ginger ale. Garnish with the squeezed lemon.

GIN DAISY

Daisies were a once popular "sour," a cocktail made tart with the addition of lemon or lime juice. The whiskey sour is the most famous of these. It was a close cousin of the fix, a sour cocktail that used pineapple syrup as a sweetener, while the Daisy used raspberry syrup or grenadine.

2 ounces gin
Juice of ½ lemon
½ teaspoon powdered sugar
1 teaspoon raspberry syrup or grenadine

Pour ingredients into an ice-filled shaker. Shake, then strain into a cocktail glass.

GIN FIZZ

2 ounces gin
Juice of ½ lemon
1 teaspoon powdered sugar (or 1 dash simple syrup)
Carbonated water
1 sprig of mint (optional)

Pour the gin, lemon juice, and sugar (or simple syrup) into a tall glass filled with ice. Top up with carbonated water. Garnish, if desired, with mint. (Adding mint makes a Southside Fizz, also known as an Alabama Fizz.)

GIN RICKEY

2 ounces gin
Juice of 1 lime
2 dashes simple syrup or maraschino liqueur
Carbonated water
Lime slice

Pour the gin, lime juice, and simple syrup (or maraschino) into an ice-filled tall glass. Top up with carbonated water. Garnish with the slice of lime.

HOFFMAN HOUSE FIZZ

3 ounces gin
Juice of ½ lemon
½ tablespoon powdered sugar (or 2 dashes simple syrup)
2 dashes maraschino liqueur
Juice of ¼ orange
1 teaspoon grenadine
Carbonated water

Pour the ingredients, except for carbonated water, into an ice-filled shaker. Shake, then strain into a highball glass. Top up with carbonated water.

IDEAL

2 ounces gin
1 ounce Italian (sweet) vermouth
3 dashes maraschino liqueur
1 dash grapefruit juice

Pour ingredients into an ice-filled shaker. Shake, then strain into a cocktail glass.

MARTINI*

3 ounces gin or vodka
French (dry) vermouth to taste
Lemon twist or olive

In an ice-filled shaker, pour ingredients in a ratio of five to one for a dry martini, or use as little as one or two drops of vermouth for an extra-dry martini. Shake, then strain into a chilled martini glass. Garnish with lemon twist or olive. Garnishing with a pickled cocktail onion makes the drink a Gibson.

MONZU

4 large mint leaves
½ ounce simple syrup
1½ ounces gin
½ ounce lime juice
¼ ounce pomegranate syrup

In a mixing glass, muddle two mint leaves in simple syrup. Add the gin, lime juice, and pomegranate syrup. Pour into an ice-filled shaker. Shake, then strain into a chilled cocktail glass. Garnish with the two remaining mint leaves.

NEGRONI

2 ounces gin
1 ounce Campari
1 ounce Italian (sweet) vermouth
Orange slice

Pour liquid ingredients into an ice-filled shaker. Shake, then strain into a cocktail glass. Garnish with the orange slice. The Negroni can be made into a long drink by straining into a tall glass and topping up with soda water.

PERFECT

An early classic, served at the old Waldorf Bar in the 1890s, and a very close cousin of the martini.

1½ ounces gin
1 ounce French (dry) vermouth
1 ounce Italian (sweet) vermouth
1 dash Angostura bitters
Twist of orange

Pour the gin and vermouth into an ice-filled shaker. Shake, then strain into a cocktail glass. Add the bitters. Garnish with the orange twist.

RAMOS GIN FIZZ*

1½ ounces gin
1 tablespoon powdered sugar (or 3 dashes simple syrup)
3–4 drops orange flower water
Juice of ½ lime
Juice of ½ lemon
1 egg white
1½ ounces cream
1 squirt seltzer
2 drops vanilla extract (optional)

Mix the ingredients in a tall bar glass, in the order listed. Add crushed ice, not too fine, since the lumps help froth the egg white. Shake for 3–4 minutes, until the mixture starts to thicken. Strain into a Collins glass.

SENSATION

3 ounces gin
1 ounce lemon juice
3 dashes maraschino liqueur
3 mint sprigs

Pour liquid ingredients into an ice-filled shaker. Shake, then strain into a cocktail glass. Garnish with the mint.

SHADY GROVE COOLER

2 ounces gin
Juice of ½ lemon
½ tablespoon sugar (or 2 dashes simple syrup)
4–5 ounces ginger beer

Pour gin and lemon juice into a tall glass filled with ice. Add sugar (or simple syrup) and stir. Top up with ginger beer.

STORK CLUB

From *The Stork Club Bar Book* (1946)

1½ ounces gin
Juice of ⅓ orange
1 dash lime juice
1 dash Cointreau
1 dash Angostura bitters

Pour ingredients into an ice-filled shaker. Shake, then strain into a cocktail glass.

TOM COLLINS

In bygone days there were many Collins drinks, all of them offshoots of the Tom Collins and the John Collins, gin sours freshened up with carbonated water. A Tom Collins called for the sweetened gin known as Old Tom gin, while a John Collins called for Holland gin.

2 ounces gin
Juice of ½ lemon
1 teaspoon powdered sugar (or 1 dash simple syrup)
Carbonated water
Lemon or orange slice

Pour the gin, lemon juice, and sugar (or simple syrup) into an ice-filled Collins glass. Top up with carbonated water. Garnish with the lemon or orange slice.

VESPER

This is the James Bond martini, named for Vesper Lynd, the doomed love interest in *Casino Royale*. "I never have more than one drink before dinner," said Bond. "But I do like that one to be very large and very strong and very cold and very well made."

3 ounces gin
1 ounce vodka
½ ounce blond Lillet
Twist of lemon

Pour liquid ingredients into an ice-filled shaker. Shake, then strain into a chilled martini glass. Garnish with the lemon twist.

RUM COCKTAILS

BERMUDA ANGLER

Invented in the 1930s by E. F. Warner, publisher of *Field & Stream*.

2 ounces amber rum
1 ounce lime juice
1 teaspoon Cointreau

Pour ingredients into an ice-filled shaker. Shake, then strain into a cocktail glass.

BETWEEN THE SHEETS

½ ounce light rum
½ ounce brandy
½ ounce lemon juice
½ ounce Cointreau

Pour ingredients into an ice-filled shaker. Shake, then strain into a cocktail glass.

BOLO

2 ounces light or amber rum
Juice of ½ lime
Juice of ¼ orange
1 teaspoon sugar (or 1 dash simple syrup)

Pour ingredients into an ice-filled shaker. Shake, then strain into a cocktail glass.

DAIQUIRI*

2 ounces light or amber rum
Juice of ½ lime
1 teaspoon sugar (or 1 dash simple syrup)

Pour ingredients into an ice-filled shaker. Shake, then strain into a cocktail glass.

DARK AND STORMY

1½ ounces Gosling's Black Seal rum
4 ounces ginger beer
Lemon or lime wedge

Pour rum over ice in a tall glass and top up with ginger beer. Squeeze a lemon or lime wedge into the drink.

EL CHICO

A favorite in the 1940s at El Chico restaurant in Greenwich Village.

1½ ounces amber rum
½ ounce Italian (sweet) vermouth
1 dash grenadine
1 dash Cointreau
1 maraschino cherry
Twist of lemon

Pour liquid ingredients into an ice-filled shaker. Shake, then strain into a cocktail glass. Garnish with the cherry and lemon twist.

EL FLORIDITA DAIQUIRI*

1¾ ounces light rum
Juice of 1 lime
2 teaspoons simple syrup
1 dash maraschino liqueur

Pour ingredients into an ice-filled shaker. Shake, then strain into a cocktail glass.

EL PRESIDENTE

1 ounce light rum
½ ounce Cointreau
½ ounce French (dry) vermouth
1 dash grenadine

Pour ingredients into an ice-filled shaker. Shake, then strain into a cocktail glass.

HONOLULU COOLER

3 ounces amber rum
1 teaspoon powdered sugar (or 1 dash simple syrup)
Juice of 1 lime
2 dashes raspberry syrup

Pour ingredients into an ice-filled shaker. Shake, then strain into a cocktail glass.

ISLE OF PINES

3 ounces light rum
1 dash grapefruit juice
1 dash lime juice

Pour ingredients into an ice-filled shaker. Shake, then strain into a cocktail glass.

KEVIN'S MANGO COLADA
Courtesy of Mango's, Anguilla, B.W.I.

1 ounce light rum
1 ounce cream of coconut
1 ounce mango juice
2 slices ripe mango
1 dash Cointreau
1 dash vanilla extract
1 pineapple stick
1 maraschino cherry
Pinch cinnamon

Shake liquid ingredients in an ice-filled shaker or blend with ice in a blender. Strain into an ice-filled highball glass. Garnish with pineapple stick and cherry. Sprinkle with cinnamon.

KOALKEEL BOMB
From the Koalkeel Restaurant, Anguilla, B.W.I.

1 ounce dark rum
2 ounces brandy
1 ounce lime juice
1 ounce simple syrup
½ ounce crème de cassis

Pour ingredients into an ice-filled shaker. Shake, then strain into a cocktail glass.

MOJITO*

The Mojito, although traditionally a long drink (it's sometimes called a Rum Collins), works just as well short. Just skip the carbonated water and pour the ingredients into a cocktail glass instead of a highball or Collins glass.

Juice of ½ lime
1 teaspoon sugar (or 1 dash simple syrup)
Mint leaves
2 ounces light or amber rum
4 ounces carbonated water
1 mint sprig

In a highball glass, muddle the lime juice and sugar with several mint leaves. Add rum, fill the glass with crushed ice, and top up with carbonated water. Garnish with a sprig of mint.

PIÑA COLADA

2 ounces amber rum
2 ounces cream of coconut
4 ounces pineapple juice
1 pineapple stick
1 maraschino cherry

Blend liquid ingredients in an electric blender with ½ cup ice until thick and smooth. Pour into a tall glass. Garnish with pineapple stick and cherry.

SANS SOUCI COOLER

Courtesy of the Sans Souci Hotel, Ocho Rios, Jamaica

1 ounce amber rum
1½ ounces pineapple juice
½ ounce orange juice
½ ounce simple syrup
1 dash lime juice
Wedge of pineapple and orange
1 maraschino cherry

Pour liquid ingredients into an ice-filled shaker. Shake, then strain into a tall glass. Garnish with the fruit.

WASHINGTON COCKTAIL

Courtesy of the Fraunces Tavern, Manhattan

1½ ounces Myers's Original Dark Rum
½ ounce lemon juice
½ ounce gin
1 dash orange juice
1 dash Cointreau
1 tablespoon sugar (or 2 dashes simple syrup)
1 maraschino cherry

Pour liquid ingredients into an ice-filled shaker. Shake, then strain into a cocktail glass. Garnish with the cherry.

CHAMPAGNE COCKTAILS

CHAMPAGNE COCKTAIL*

1 sugar cube
Angostura bitters
4 ounces chilled champagne
Twist of lemon

Place the sugar cube in a chilled champagne flute and moisten with a few dashes of bitters. Add champagne. Garnish with the lemon twist.

CHAMPEARMINT

From the Mark Hotel, Manhattan

1 ounce pear brandy (Poire William)
1 dash vodka
4 ounces chilled champagne
1 slice fresh pear
2 mint leaves
1 dash white crème de menthe

Pour brandy and vodka into a chilled champagne flute. Top up with champagne. Garnish with the pear slice and mint leaves. Pour dash of crème de menthe over pear slice.

KIR ROYALE 38

From La Caravelle Restaurant, Manhattan

1 teaspoon cognac
1 teaspoon Grand Marnier
4 ounces champagne
½ orange slice

Pour the cognac and Grand Marnier into a chilled champagne flute. Top up with champagne. Garnish with the orange slice.

LE PERROQUET

A signature drink in years gone by at Le Perroquet Restaurant, Chicago.

2 ounces orange juice
1 dash gin
1 large dash Campari
4 ounces chilled champagne
Twists of orange and lemon

Pour orange juice, gin, and Campari into a chilled champagne flute. Top up with champagne. Garnish with the twists of orange and lemon.

PARK AVENUE

From *The Stork Club Bar Book* (1946)

1 ounce brandy
¼ ounce Grand Marnier
4 ounces chilled champagne

Pour brandy and Grand Marnier into a chilled champagne flute. Top up with champagne.

PICK-ME-UP

Created by Georges Melitz, the Ritz, Paris.

2 ounces orange juice
1 ounce brandy
1 ounce Cointreau
4 ounces chilled champagne

Pour the orange juice, brandy, and Cointreau into an ice-filled shaker. Shake, then strain into a chilled champagne flute. Top up with champagne.

POUSSE L'AMOUR

1 ounce chilled armagnac
½ ounce orange juice
1 dash Cointreau
4 ounces chilled champagne
Orange slice

Pour the armagnac and orange juice into a champagne flute, add Cointreau, and top up with champagne. Garnish with the orange slice.

VODKA COCKTAILS

BARTENDER'S BREAKFAST

From the Zeta Bar, London

2 medium plum tomatoes
1 ounce lemon juice
1½ ounces lemon vodka
½ ounce dry (fino) sherry
1 teaspoon chopped basil
1 teaspoon chopped cilantro
1 teaspoon chopped chives
2 dashes jalapeno Tabasco
1 large dash Worcestershire sauce
Pinch salt

Large pinch celery salt
Good grinding of black pepper
2 celery sticks (for garnish)

Blend the tomatoes and lemon juice in a blender. Add the rest of the ingredients (except the celery sticks). Pour into an ice-filled shaker. Shake, then strain into a tall glass. Garnish with the celery sticks.

BILLIE HOLIDAY

From the Time Cafe, Manhattan

$2\frac{1}{2}$ ounces orange vodka
$1\frac{1}{2}$ ounces blue curaçao
$\frac{1}{2}$ ounce pineapple juice
$\frac{1}{2}$ ounce cranberry juice
$\frac{1}{2}$ ounce lime juice
Twist of lemon

Pour liquid ingredients into an ice-filled shaker. Shake, then strain into a chilled martini glass. Garnish with the lemon twist.

BLOOD ORANGE MARTINI

From the Cub Room, Manhattan

3 ounces orange vodka
$\frac{1}{2}$ ounce Campari
$\frac{1}{2}$ ounce orange juice

Pour ingredients into an ice-filled shaker. Shake, then strain into a chilled martini glass.

BLOODY MARY*

I prefer the slow, steady fire of Stolichnaya's Pertsovka, but Absolut Peppar has a fresh jalapeno note that makes for a Tex-Mex Bloody Mary.

3 ounces pepper vodka
4 ounces V-8 juice
Juice of 1 lemon wedge

Juice of 1 lime wedge
1 dash Worcestershire sauce
Pinch celery salt
Salt and pepper
Celery stalk

Mix the ingredients (except the celery stalk) in a tall, ice-filled glass. Garnish with the celery stalk.

THE BLOOMS

3 ounces vodka
4 ounces tomato juice
$\frac{1}{2}$ teaspoon horseradish
$\frac{1}{8}$ teaspoon Dijon mustard
$\frac{1}{8}$ teaspoon Tabasco
Juice of 1 lemon
Pinch Old Bay seasoning
Salt and pepper

Pour liquid ingredients into a tall, ice-filled glass. Add the seasonings and stir.

GREEN EYE-OPENER

A signature drink at the old Sign of the Dove, Manhattan.

$1\frac{1}{2}$ ounces vodka
1 dash Rose's lime juice
2 ounces orange juice
1 dash blue curaçao
1 dash Cointreau
Celery salt
Salt and pepper
Celery stalk

Pour liquid ingredients into a tall, ice-filled glass. Add celery salt, salt, and pepper to taste, and stir with the celery stalk.

LEMON VODKA MARTINI

2 ounces lemon vodka
2 or 3 drops Cointreau
Twist of lemon

Pour liquid ingredients into an ice-filled shaker. Shake, then strain into a chilled martini glass. Garnish with the lemon twist.

MOSCOW MULE

The Moscow Mule should have been called the Trojan Horse, since its sole purpose was to get Americans in the 1940s to drink vodka. It was at the heart of a massive advertising campaign by Smirnoff. Despite the dubious origins, the drink makes a nice summer cooler.

3 ounces vodka
1 12-ounce bottle ginger beer
Juice of $\frac{1}{2}$ lime
Wedge of lime

Pour the liquid ingredients into a tall, ice-filled glass. Garnish with the lime wedge.

SALTY DOG

1 lime wedge
Sugar
Salt
2 ounces vodka
4 ounces grapefruit juice

Moisten the rim of an old-fashioned glass with the lime wedge, then dip the rim in a mixture of equal parts sugar and salt. Pour liquid ingredients into an ice-filled shaker. Shake, then strain into the glass. Garnish with the lime wedge.

SILVERADO

1½ ounces vodka
1½ ounces Campari
1½ ounces orange juice

Pour ingredients into an ice-filled shaker. Shake, then strain into a cocktail glass.

TEQUILA COCKTAILS

ARIZONA LEMONADE

From the restaurant Arizona 206, Manhattan

2 ounces gold tequila
8 ounces fresh lemonade, slightly sweet
Lemon wheel

Pour liquid ingredients into a tall, ice-filled glass. Garnish with the lemon.

MARGARITA

1 lime wedge
Kosher salt
2 ounces tequila
½ ounce Cointreau
Juice of ½ lime

Moisten the rim of a chilled cocktail glass with the lime wedge, then dip the rim in salt. Pour liquid ingredients into an ice-filled shaker. Shake, then strain into the glass. Garnish with the lime wedge.

TEQUILA SUNRISE

1½ ounces tequila
¾ ounce grenadine
4 ounces orange juice

Pour ingredients into an ice-filled shaker. Shake, then strain into a cocktail glass.

WINE AND VERMOUTH COCKTAILS

ADONIS

Adonis opened at the Opera House in Manhattan on September 9, 1884, and became the first Broadway musical to run for more than 500 performances. It inspired this cocktail, which was served at the old Waldorf Bar. I have substituted for orange bitters.

1½ ounces dry (fino) sherry
½ ounce Italian (sweet) vermouth
2 dashes Angostura bitters
Twist of orange

Pour liquid ingredients into an ice-filled shaker. Shake, then strain into a cocktail glass. Garnish with the orange twist.

BAMBOO

The Bamboo, which dates back to the nineteenth century, is one of many cocktails that called for orange bitters. I have substituted Angostura bitters and a twist of orange.

2 ounces dry sherry
¾ ounce French (dry) vermouth
1 dash Angostura bitters (optional)
Twist of orange

Pour liquid ingredients into an ice-filled shaker. Shake, then strain into a cocktail glass. Garnish with the orange twist.

CORONATION

This cocktail won second prize in a 1903 contest sponsored by the *Police Gazette*. It calls for orange bitters, for which I have substituted a twist of orange and Angostura bitters.

$3\frac{1}{2}$ ounces dry (fino) sherry
$\frac{1}{2}$ ounce French (dry) vermouth
1 dash maraschino liqueur
1 dash Angostura bitters
Olive
Twist of orange
Twist of lemon

Pour liquid ingredients into an ice-filled shaker. Shake, then strain into a cocktail glass. Garnish with the olive and the orange and lemon twists.

TRILBY

3 ounces French (dry) vermouth
1 dash Cointreau
1 dash Peychaud's bitters
$\frac{1}{2}$ ounce whiskey
Twist of lemon

Pour vermouth, Cointreau, and bitters into an ice-filled shaker. Shake, then strain into a cocktail glass. Pour the whiskey on top. Garnish with the lemon twist.

VERMOUTH CASSIS

3 ounces French (dry) vermouth
1 ounce crème de cassis
Carbonated water
Twist of lemon

Pour liquid ingredients into an ice-filled shaker. Shake, then strain into a cocktail glass. Garnish with the lemon twist.

VERMOUTH COCKTAIL

3 ounces French (dry) vermouth
1 dash Cointreau
2 dashes Angostura bitters
Twist of lemon

Pour liquid ingredients into an ice-filled shaker. Shake, then strain into a cocktail glass. Garnish with the lemon twist.

EXOTIC COCKTAILS
(COCKTAILS BASED ON AN INGREDIENT NOT IN THE ABOVE CATEGORIES)

AMERICANO

You can make this drink short or long. Short for an aperitif, long for a summer cooler.

2 ounces Campari
½ ounce Italian (sweet) vermouth
Carbonated water
Orange wheel

Pour Campari and vermouth into an ice-filled shaker. Shake, then strain into a cocktail glass. Top up with carbonated water. Garnish with the orange wheel.

CASSIS HIGHBALL

1 ounce crème de cassis
2 dashes Angostura bitters
4 ounces carbonated water

Pour the crème de cassis and bitters into an ice-filled highball glass. Top up with carbonated water and stir.

JEFFERSON PIMM'S CUP

Adapted from the Jefferson Hotel, Washington, D.C.

2 ounces Pimm's No. 1 Cup
2 ounces ginger beer
Carbonated water
1 mint sprig
1 cucumber slice
Twist of orange
1 maraschino cherry

Pour Pimm's and ginger beer into a tall, ice-filled glass. Top up with carbonated water. Stir. Garnish with mint, cucumber, orange twist, and cherry.

PARLOR PUNCH

From Lafcadio Hearn's *La Cuisine Créole* (1885)

6 ounces English black tea, chilled
3 ounces whiskey
1½ ounces dark rum
1 tablespoon sugar (or 3 dashes simple syrup)
1 dash lemon juice
1 dash raspberry syrup

Pour ingredients into an ice-filled shaker. Shake, then strain into a cocktail glass.

ROSALIND RUSSELL

Rosalind Russell gave this recipe to the author of *The Stork Club Bar Book* (1946).

2 ounces aquavit
1 ounce French (dry) vermouth or blond Dubonnet

Pour ingredients into an ice-filled shaker. Shake, then strain into a cocktail glass.

SAKETINI

From Mirezi Restaurant, Manhattan

1–2 ounces sake
4–5 ounces vodka
1 slice unpeeled cucumber

Pour liquid ingredients into an ice-filled shaker. Shake, then strain into a chilled martini glass. Garnish with the cucumber slice.

THE UNEXPECTED

From Basil's Bar and Restaurant, Mustique, B.W.I.

1 ounce Cointreau
1 dash lime or lemon juice
4 ounces carbonated water

Pour the Cointreau and lime or lemon juice into an ice-filled highball glass. Top up with carbonated water and stir.

VENETIAN SUNSET

From Felidia Restaurant, Manhattan

1 ounce grappa
4 ounces orange juice
1 ounce cranberry juice
2 mint leaves

Pour ingredients into an ice-filled shaker. Shake, then strain into a cocktail glass. Garnish with the mint leaves.

BIBLIOGRAPHY

A complete listing of pre-1910 bartender's manuals and other books containing cocktail recipes can be found on a Web site maintained by Lowell Edmunds, the author of *Martini, Straight Up* and *The Silver Bullet*. The address is www-rci.rutgers.edu/~edmunds/barman.html.

Adams, Ramon. *Western Words*. Norman: University of Oklahoma Press, 1968.

Ade, George. *The Old-Time Saloon*. New York: Long & Smith, 1931.

Altschul, Ira D. *Drinks as They Were Made Before Prohibition*. Santa Barbara, Cal.: Schauer Printing Studio, 1934.

Amis, Kingsley. *On Drink*. London: Jonathan Cape, 1972.

Arthur, Stanley Clisby. *Famous New Orleans Drinks and How to Mix 'Em*. New Orleans: Harmanson, 1937.

Baker, Charles H., Jr. *The Gentleman's Companion. Vol. 1, Being an Exotic Drinking Book*. New York: Crown, 1946.

Barkeeper's Ready Reference. St. Louis: Bevill, 1871.

Bartender's Guide: How to Mix Drinks. Milwaukee: Royal, 1914.

Bartlett, John Russell. *Dictionary of Americanisms*, 4th ed. Boston: Little, Brown, 1877.

Barty-King, Hugh, and Anton Massel. *Rum: Yesterday and Today*. London: Heinemann, 1983.

Bayles, W. Harrison. *Old Taverns of New York*. New York: Frank Allaben Genealogical Co., 1915.

166 BIBLIOGRAPHY

4ment
Beebe, Lucius. *The Stork Club Bar Book*. New York: Rinehart, 1946.

Bergeron, Victor J. *Trader Vic's Bartender's Guide*. Garden City, N.Y.: Doubleday, 1972.

Berrey, Lester V., and Melvin van den Bark. *The American Thesaurus of Slang*, 2nd ed. New York: Crowell, 1953.

Berry, Jeff, and Annene Kaye. *Beachbum Berry's Grog Log*. San Jose: SLG Publishing, 1998.

Birmingham, Frederic A., ed. *Esquire Drink Book*. New York: Harper & Brothers, 1956.

Boothby, William T. *Cocktail Boothby's American Bartender*. San Francisco: San Francisco News Co., 1891.

Bredenbek, Magnus. *What Shall We Drink?: Popular Drinks, Recipes, and Toasts*. New York: Carlyle House, 1934.

Bridenbaugh, Carl. *Cities in Revolt: Urban Life in America, 1743–1776*. New York: Knopf, 1955.

———. *Cities in the Wilderness: The First Century of Urban Life in America, 1625–1742*. New York: Ronald Press, 1938.

Brooks, Johnny. *My 35 Years Behind Bars*. New York: Exposition Press, 1954.

Brown, John Hull. *Early American Beverages*. Rutland, Vt.: C. E. Tuttle, 1966.

Buñuel, Luis. *My Last Sigh*. New York: Vintage, 1984.

Byron, O. H. *The Modern Bartender's Guide*. New York: Excelsior, 1884.

Carson, Gerald. *Rum and Reform in Old New England*. Sturbridge, Mass.: Old Sturbridge Inc., 1966.

———. *The Social History of Bourbon*. New York: Dodd, Mead, 1963.

Chayette, Hervé, and Alain Weill. *Les cocktails*. Paris: Editions Nathan, 1988.

Cobb, Irvin S. *Irvin S. Cobb's Own Recipe Book*. Louisville: Frankfort Distilleries, 1936.

Conrad, Barnaby, III. *Absinthe*. San Francisco: Chronicle Books, 1988.

———. *The Martini*. San Francisco: Chronicle Books, 1995.

Craddock, Harry. *The Savoy Cocktail Book*. London: Constable, 1930.

Crahan, Marcus. *Early American Inebrietatis*. Los Angeles: Zamorano Club, 1964.

Craigie, Sir William A. *A Dictionary of American English on Historical Principles*, vols. 1–4. Chicago: University of Chicago Press, 1959.

Crockett, Albert Stevens. *The Old Waldorf-Astoria Bar Book*. New York: Dodd, Mead, 1934.

————. *Old Waldorf Bar Days*. New York: Aventine Press, 1931.

Crowgey, Henry G. *Kentucky Bourbon: The Early Years of Whiskey Making*. Lexington: University of Kentucky Press, 1972.

Dabney, Joseph Earl. *Mountain Spirits*. New York: Scribner's, 1974.

De Gouy, Louis P. *The Cocktail Hour*. New York: Greenberg, 1951.

DeVoto, Bernard. *The Hour*. Boston: Riverside Press, 1948.

Donohoe, Robert W. *Martini Hotline: A Ten-Year Journey*. Athens, Ohio: privately printed, 1998.

Dorchester, Daniel. *The Liquor Problem in All Ages*. New York: Phillips and Hunt, 1888.

Doxat, John. *Stirred—Not Shaken: The Dry Martini*. London: Hutchinson Benham, 1976.

————. *The World of Drinks and Drinking*. New York: Drake, 1972.

DuBrow, Maxwell. *Cocktails for Two Thousand*. New York: Elizabeth Norman Restaurant, 1951.

Duffy, Patrick Gavin. *The Official Mixer's Manual*. New York: Long & Smith, 1934.

Durrell, Edward Henry ("Henry Didimus"). *New Orleans As I Found It*. New York: Harper & Brothers, 1845.

Earle, Alice M. *Customs and Fashions in Old New England*. New York: Scribner's, 1902.

————. *Home Life in Colonial Days*. New York: Macmillan, 1906.

————. "Old Colonial Drinks and Drinkers." *National Magazine* 16 (June 1892).

————. *Stage-coach and Tavern Days*. New York: Macmillan, 1900.

Edmunds, Lowell. *Martini, Straight Up: The Classic American Cocktail*. Baltimore: Johns Hopkins University Press, 1998.

————. *The Silver Bullet: The Martini in American Civilization*. Westport, Conn.: Greenwood Press, 1981.

Edwards, Bill. *How to Mix Drinks*. Philadelphia: David McKay, 1936.

Embury, David A. *The Fine Art of Mixing Drinks*. Garden City, N.Y.: Doubleday, 1948.

Emerson, Edward R. *Beverages Past and Present*, vols. 1–2. New York: Putnam's, 1908.

Engel, Leo. *American and Other Drinks*. London: Tinsley Bros., 1880.

Ensslin, Hugo R. *Recipes for Mixed Drinks*. New York: Ensslin, 1916.

Esquire's Handbook for Hosts. New York: Grosset & Dunlap, 1949.

Farmer, John S. *Americanisms—Old and New*. London: Poulter, 1889.

Feery, William C. *Wet Drinks for Dry People*. Chicago: Bazner Press, 1932.

Field, Edward. *The Colonial Tavern*. Providence, R.I.: Preston and Rounds, 1897.

Field, S. S. *The American Drink Book*. New York: Farrar, Straus and Young, 1953.

Fleischmann, Joseph. *The Art of Blending and Compounding Liquors and Wines*. Danbury, Conn.: Behrens, 1885.

Fougner, G. Selmer. *Along the Wine Trail*, vols. 1–5. New York: New York Sun, 1934–36. Contains reprinted columns, many of them on cocktails, written for the *New York Sun*.

———. *Baron Fougner's Bar Guide*. Detroit: n.p., 1940.

Francatelli, Charles. *The Cook's Guide and Housekeeper's and Butler's Assistant*. London: Bentley, 1863. Has a chapter on American drinks.

Furnas, J. C. *The Life and Times of the Late Demon Rum*. New York: Putnam's, 1965.

Gaige, Crosby. *Crosby Gaige's Cocktail Guide and Lady's Companion*. New York: Barrows, 1941.

———. *The Standard Cocktail Guide*. New York: M. Barrows, 1944.

Getz, Oscar. *Whiskey: An American Pictorial History*. New York: McKay, 1978.

Giggle Water. New York: Warnock, 1928.

Gorman, Marion, and Felipe P. de Alba. *The Tequila Book*. Chicago: Regnery, 1976.

Grohusko, Jacob. *Jack's Manual*. New York: Knopf, 1933.

Guyer, William, ed. *The Merry Mixer*. New York: Pepper, 1933.

Haimo, Oscar. *Cocktail and Wine Digest*. New York: n.p., 1945.

Hall, Basil. *Travels in North America in the Years 1827 and 1828*, vols. 1–3. Edinburgh, 1829.

Haney, Jesse. *Haney's Steward and Barkeeper's Manual*. New York: Jesse Haney, 1869.

Harwell, Richard B. *The Mint Julep*. Charlottesville: University Press of Virginia, 1975.

Haywood, Joseph L. *Mixology: The Art of Preparing All Kinds of Drinks*. Wilmington: Press of the Sunday Star, 1898.

Herzbrun, Robert. *The Perfect Martini Book*. New York: Harcourt Brace Jovanovich, 1979.

Hirschfeld, Al. *Manhattan Oases*. New York: Dutton, c. 1932.

Hoffmann, Henry. *The "Count" Reminisces*. St. Louis: Hoffmann and Kurz, 1933.

Holbrook, Stewart H. *Far Corner: A Personal View of the Pacific Northwest*. New York: Macmillan, 1952.

Hooker, Richard J. *Food and Drink in America.* Indianapolis: Bobbs Merrill, 1981.

Janson, Charles William. *The Stranger in America, 1793–1806.* New York: Press of the Pioneers, 1935.

Jillson, Willard Rouse. *Early Kentucky Distillers.* Louisville: Standard Printing, 1940.

Johnson, Byron A., and Sharon Peregrine Johnson. *The Authentic Guide to Drinks of the Civil War Era, 1853–1873.* Gettysburg, Pa., 1992.

———. *Wild West Bartenders' Bible.* Austin: Texas Monthly Press, 1986.

Johnson, Harry. *Bartender's Manual.* New York: Samisch & Goldmann, 1882.

"Judge, Jr." *Here's How!* New York: Leslie Judge Co., 1927.

Kappeler, George J. *Modern American Drinks.* New York: Merriam, 1895.

Keller, Mark, and Mairi McCormick. *A Dictionary of Words About Alcohol.* New Brunswick, N.J.: Publications Division, Rutgers Center of Alcohol Studies, 1968.

Kobler, John. *Ardent Spirits: The Rise and Fall of Prohibition.* New York: Putnam's, 1973.

Krout, John A. *The Origins of Prohibition.* New York: Knopf, 1925.

Lamore, Harry. *The New Police Gazette Bartenders Guide.* New York: Richard K. Fox, 1901.

Lawlor, Christopher F. *The Mixologist.* Cincinnati: Clarke, 1895.

Lender, Mark Edward, and James Kirby Martin. *Drinking in America.* New York: Free Press, 1982.

Lynde, Benjamin. *The Diaries of Benjamin Lynde and of Benjamin Lynde, Jr.* Cambridge, Mass.: Riverside Press, 1880.

McCusker, John J. *Rum and the American Revolution.* New York: Garland, 1989.

MacElhone, Harry. *Barflies and Cocktails.* Paris: Lecram Press, 1927.

———. *Harry's ABC of Mixing Cocktails.* London: Souvenir Press, 1986. First published 1919.

Marryat, Frederick. *A Diary in America.* Bloomington: Indiana University Press, 1968.

Mason, Dexter. *The Art of Drinking, or What to Make with What You Have.* New York: Farrar & Rinehart, 1930.

Mayabb, James. *International Cocktail Specialties.* New York: Hearthside Press, 1962.

Meier, Frank. *The Artistry of Mixing Drinks.* Paris: Fryam Press, 1936.

Mencken, Henry L. *The American Language.* New York: Knopf, 1937; Supplement I (1945); Supplement II (1948).

————. *Happy Days.* New York: Knopf, 1940.

————. *Tall Tales and Hoaxes of H. L. Mencken.* Ed. John W. Baer. Annapolis: Franklin Printing, 1990.

Mew, James, and John Ashton. *Drinks of the World.* London: Leadenhall Press, 1892.

Michaux, François André. *Travels to the Westward of the Allegheny Mountains.* London: J. Mawman, 1805.

Montague, Harry. *The Up-to-Date Bartender's Guide.* Ottenheimer, 1913.

Monzert, Leonard. *The Independent Liquorist.* New York: Dick & Fitzgerald, 1866.

Mueller, Charles C. *Pioneers of Mixing.* New York: Trinity Press, 1934. Described on title page as "Collection of recipes from the log of American traveling mixicologists."

Noling, A. W. *Beverage Literature: A Bibliography.* Metuchen, N.J.: Scarecrow Press, 1971.

One Hundred Famous Cocktails. New York: Kenilworth Press, 1934. "Published in collaboration with Oscar of the Waldorf."

Orton, Vrest. *The American Cider Book.* New York: Farrar, Straus and Giroux, 1973.

Peke, Hewson L. *Americana Ebrietatis.* New York, 1917.

Porter, Henry, and George Roberts. *Cups and Their Customs.* London, 1869.

Powner, Willard. *The Complete Bartender's Guide.* Chicago: Powner, 1934.

Proskauer, Julien J. *What'll You Have?* New York: Burt, 1934.

Rawling, Ernest P. *Rawling's Book of Mixed Drinks.* San Francisco: Guild Press, 1914.

Regan, Gary, and Mary Haidin Regan. *The Book of Bourbon and Other Fine American Whiskeys.* Shelburne, Vt.: Chapters Publishing, 1995.

————. *The Martini Companion: A Connoisseur's Guide.* Philadelphia: Running Press, 1997.

Reibstein, August. *"Mixology": Recipes for Old and New Mixed Drinks.* New York: Reibstein, 1933.

Reinhardt, Charles Nicholas. *"Cheerio!"* New York: Elf, 1928. Author identified as "Charles, formerly of Delmonico's."

Root, Waverley, and Richard de Rochemont. *Eating in America: A History.* New York: Ecco, 1981.

Rorabaugh, W. J. *The Alcoholic Republic: An American Tradition.* New York: Oxford University Press, 1979.

Schmidt, A. William ("The Only William"). *The Flowing Bowl.* New York: Webster, 1892.

Scientific Bar-Keeping. Buffalo, N.Y.: Cook, 1884.

Seldes, Gilbert. *The Future of Drinking.* Boston: Little, Brown, 1930.

Stuart, Thomas. *Stuart's Fancy Drinks and How to Mix Them.* New York: Excelsior, 1896.

Sullivan, Jere. *The Drinks of Yesteryear: A Mixology.* Privately printed, 1930.

Swan, Fred W. *When Good Fellows Get Together (Drink and Service Manual).* Chicago: Reilly & Lee, 1933.

Terrington, William. *Cooling Cups and Dainty Drinks.* London: Routledge, 1869.

Thomas, Jerry. *How to Mix Drinks, or The Bon-Vivant's Companion.* New York: Dick & Fitzgerald, 1862.

Thornton, Richard H. *An American Glossary.* Philadelphia: Lippincott, 1912.

Torelli, Adolphe. *900 recettes de cocktails et boissons américaines.* Paris: Bornemann, 1930.

Townshend, Jack. *The Bartender's Book.* New York: Viking, 1951.

Toye, Nina, and A. H. Adair. *Drinks, Long and Short.* London: Heinemann, 1925.

Valentine's Manual of Old New York. New York: Valentine's Manual, Inc., 1923, 1926, 1927.

Victorian Cups and Punches, and Other Concoctions. London: Cassell, 1974. Has material on American drinks.

Walker, Danton. *Guide to New York Night Life.* New York: Putnam's, 1958.

Weiss, Harry. *The History of Applejack or Apple Brandy in New Jersey from Colonial Times to the Present.* Trenton, N.J.: New Jersey Agricultural Society, 1954.

West, Elliot. *The Saloon on the Rocky Mountain Mining Frontier.* Lincoln, Neb., 1979.

Wiley, James A., with Helene M. Griffith. *The Art of Mixing.* Philadelphia: Macrae Smith, 1932.

Willkie, H. F. *Beverage Spirits in America: A Brief History.* New York: Newcomen Society of England, American Branch, 1949.

Woon, Basil Dillon. *When It's Cocktail Time in Cuba.* New York: Liveright, 1928.

ACKNOWLEDGMENTS

Since the first edition of this book appeared, the lonely field of cocktail history has become a little more populated, and I have profited by the comments, suggestions, and tips of several dedicated writers and historians. These include Lowell Edmunds, the first and still preeminent scholar in the field he single-handedly created, "bacchanology"; Gary Regan, the editor of ardentspirits.com; the tireless Ted Haigh ("Dr. Cocktail"); David Wondrich of *Esquire*; and J. F. Hansman, formerly of Cambridge University, where he took time from teaching archaeology to research the equally important field of drink. Dale DeGroff, the Jerry Thomas of the present age, has been a valuable resource. Susan Scott, archivist for the Savoy Hotel, provided valuable information on the Savoy bar. And as before, I thank Anita Leclerc, who got me started writing about cocktails many years ago at *Esquire*.

INDEX

Numbers in **bold type** refer to recipes.